Also by Carlo Gébler

NOVELS

The Eleventh Summer

August in July

Work and Play

Malachy and His Family

Life of a Drum

The Cure

How to Murder a Man

A Good Day for a Dog

The Dead Eight

The Innocent of Falkland Road

I, Antigone

SHORT FICTION

W9 and Other Lives

The Wing Orderly's Tales

Aesop's Fables: The Cruelty of the Gods (with Gavin Weston)

Dark Tales from Fermanagh (with Seamas McCanny)

Tales We Tell Ourselves: A Selection from the Decameron

MEMOIR

Father and I: A Memoir

Confessions of a Catastrophist

The Projectionist: The Story of Ernest Gébler

NON-FICTION

Driving Through Cuba: An East–West Journey

The Glass Curtain: Inside an Ulster Community

The Siege of Derry

My Father's Watch: The Story of a Child Prisoner in 70s Britain (with Patrick Maguire)

A Cold Eye: Notes from a Shared Island, 1989–2024

YOUNG ADULT

Caught on a Train

August '44

Frozen Out

The Bull Raid

CHILDREN

The TV Genie

The Witch That Wasn't

The Base

PLAYS

Dance of Death

10 Rounds

Henry and Harriet: And Other Plays

Belfast by Moonlight

Walking to the Ark

NO ONE TELLS YOU

The Last Years of Edna O'Brien

Carlo Gébler

NEW ISLAND

NO ONE TELLS YOU
First published in 2026 by
New Island Books
Glenshesk House
10 Richview Office Park
Clonskeagh
Dublin D14 V8C4
Republic of Ireland
www.newisland.ie

Print ISBN: 978-1-83594-057-0
eBook ISBN: 978-1-83594-062-4

British Library Cataloguing in Publication Data. A CIP catalogue record for this book is available from the British Library.

Product safety queries can be addressed to New Island Books at the above postal address or at info@newisland.ie.

Set in Adobe Caslon Pro in 11 on 16pt
Typeset by Palimpsest Book Production Limited, Falkirk, Stirlingshire
Cover design by Luke Bird, lukebird.co.uk
Printed by Scandbook, scandbook.com

the arts council an chomhairle ealaíon funding literature

FSC www.fsc.org MIX Paper | Supporting responsible forestry FSC® C021394

New Island received financial assistance from The Arts Council (An Chomhairle Ealaíon), Dublin, Ireland.

New Island Books is a member of Publishing Ireland and the Independent Publishers Guild.

10 9 8 7 6 5 4 3 2 1

Author's Note

This is a work of non-fiction. It is a personal account with a singular point of view. The experience of others will be quite different. Despite reliance on diaries and other records, errors of recall are inevitable but never intentional. Some names have been changed.

I would like to thank Dermot Bolger, Lee Brackstone, Christine Breen, Maya Kulukundis, Nicky Shulman, Philip St John and Djinn von Noorden for their encouragement and advice.

I was corresponding with my old friend Nicky. She had known my mother, the writer Edna O'Brien, since the 1970s and asked how she was. I said she was dying. Nicky wrote back instantly, 'I thought she was eternal.'

Yes, I thought when I read this. Yes.

This was one of those bedrock truths that are so rarely gifted. There was nothing that should be cut and there was nothing to add to it, either. 'I thought she was eternal.' That was exactly how she seemed. Or had.

It was July 2024 when Nicky wrote. I was at home in County Fermanagh. My mother was living in London. The weather in Ireland was grey and the skies were overcast. At night, when I clambered into bed, the sheets felt vaguely damp.

I walked most days, tramping along lanes with high unruly hedgerows; the air smelt of honeysuckle and molasses. These were silage-making times. In my mind though, I was back in London in the winter of 1958, just after we moved there from Ireland when I was four, and I was in our new suburban house, cold and comfortless unlike the home we'd left behind in Dublin, or I was out on Cannon Hill Common, which our new domicile overlooked, with my parents and my younger brother, walking. There were two smells on the Common; the odour of decayed leaves and the chemical tang of the spent fireworks that littered the ground – it was early November, just after Guy Fawkes Night and the scorched cardboard carcasses of fireworks were everywhere – and walking the Fermanagh lanes I could smell what I'd smelt then again, the heavy pall of leaf mulch, the stinging odour of saltpetre.

In Ireland that July persistent memories of childhood places kept arising unbidden, and along with them I was plagued by knowing what was coming – my mother's death. It was like a sore tooth to which the tongue keeps darting: it wouldn't let me alone and I couldn't keep away from it either. It was in my dreams. And when I woke in the morning it was the first thing I thought about.

That summer I was following my habitual routine. I went to the study every day to write. I've always been able to manage that, whatever the circumstances, but when I read the words that I'd written back they had no heft, no lift. Now and again, however, I set aside what I thought I should be writing, and I let the tongue go to the sore tooth and I wrote about that and when I did the words streamed out with purposefulness and relief. And when I read them back, I felt the presence of heft and lift. After this had happened a few times, I decided I should stick with the sore tooth. I would write about my experience of my mother's death. It was what I needed to do. Solipsistic of course, but it had to be done.

For a long time, my mother's health had been failing. The clockwork motor was in decline, as she sometimes put it, and for a decade if not longer, she had regularly issued bulletins with basic information about her condition. The bulletins on her cancer were the most meagre of all her communiqués. She never disclosed the nature, type or provenance of whatever hers was. We never talked about 'it'. Chemo was only occasionally mentioned in passing. There was none of the openness, say, that David Rieff describes in *Swimming in a Sea of Death*, his account of his experience of his mother Susan Sontag's death from cancer. Rieff's book opens with an account of going with Sontag to the oncologist, Dr A. The medic's prognosis is bleak and when he finishes, his devastated patient sums up the situation by saying, 'So what you're telling me . . . is that in fact there is nothing to be done.'[1] Such an encounter would never

1 David Rieff, *Swimming in a Sea of Death* (London: Granta, 2008), p. 14.

have happened with my mother. That just wasn't her way. An Irish countrywoman's reserve, like her mother and probably all the mothers who came before her mother – that was her default.

All this reticence was welcomed by my death-denying side, which is very strongly developed. Mmm, I would say to myself as we both aged, she with a 24-year head start on me, her death is far, far away. Oh, how easy it is to believe what we want, and I've had a lifetime to master my own practice here.

And then, of course, the day came when it wasn't theoretical, which is where I start.

2020

The first Saturday of May. I was in my study when I received an email from my mother. A long one. She had written it in her house in Ovington Street in Chelsea, where she had been living for many years. It was about her Friday night, which was *the night before.* Whatever else was going on in her life, I thought before I read on, at least the legendary capacity to transmute experience into language with phenomenal alacrity was still there, still functioning.

'I am lucky to be alive,' she began. There was an opener to command attention.

'Last evening,' she continued, 'I was cooking a bit of pasta.'

The pasta was baking in the oven in the kitchen, she explained, and she was working in the dining room next door. She was working on 'The Leap', a lecture on T. S. Eliot she'd been commissioned to deliver on her birthday, 15 December 2020. This was to be the fifth in a series of annual lectures by different speakers on T. S. Eliot. These lectures are commissioned by the T. S. Eliot Foundation and presented at the Abbey Theatre in Dublin.

To help the writing, she explained, she had lit a candle 'for luck and to help see the text'. I could picture the scene – the candle in its holder with its trembling flame, the manuscript pages washed in pale yellow light.

She left the table and went to the kitchen to see to her dinner. At that moment 'the kitchen fire alarm goes off', she wrote, 'and I think it's [the] oven [timer] and pull the pasta out'. But the alarm rang on, 'getting worse' as she put it. Thinking then it was the central heating boiler alarm she was hearing, she 'ran' down to the basement. The boiler's alarm was not sounding and so she 'ran' back upstairs and this was when she realised it was the smoke alarm she'd been hearing all along, because 'there on the dining table is a sea of flame (my writing and papers etc.) and I run into the street where two young people, total strangers, are going by'.

The strangers in the street were a couple. My mother brought them into the house. The 'girl' got towels to damp down the flames (I could visualise the bathroom upstairs at the back of the house with the deep blue walls where she got them from) while the 'man' rang the fire brigade. Three or four minutes later a tender pulled up and several firemen rushed in through the front door with hoses and put out the fire raging on the dining-room table, destroying in the process the pages on Eliot on which she'd been labouring for months. Every writer's nightmare. The hand-written first draft lost to fire and to water.

Two of the firemen sat her on a chair (one was Irish, she later told me on the telephone though I forgot to ask which county, and his accent consoled her). She was given oxygen and draped in what she called 'a strange foil covering to reduce shock'. Some of her neighbours saw the tender parked in the street and came in through the open front door to do the neighbourly thing. The firemen left. The crisis had passed. Her house was still standing even if her work had perished.

Her email noted that – now time had passed since Friday evening – she had processed what she called 'the full extent of it'. What now hit her most, she said, was that it had been 'an utter miracle that those two people were passing by' when she ran out because other than this amorous couple the street was 'deserted', as was to be expected because of Covid. No one was around. Without them the fire would have raged and more than her manuscript pages would have been consumed. Some or even all of her house would have gone up too. Without the good luck of the couple, it might have been, could have been, no, *would* have been, a catastrophe. That, I understood, was what she meant.

In the email's middle came practical counsel; she liked to salt her emails with advice and often it was very good. 'I hope you have fire alarms in your various rooms,' she wrote, 'and never leave lit candles unless you are there.' Then she qualified. She recognised it 'was a freak accident' but added 'that's what happens', inferring that when candles and manuscript papers were brought together, fires followed. This made fire alarms – I think this instruction was really for her, who was always lighting candles, rather than for me – even more necessary. But, of course, she wouldn't ever again leave a candle burning alone in a room. That was the lesson learned.

At the very end of her email, she adverted to the clean-up. 'A little girl' (I don't know who this was – the girl from the street who got the towels or someone else?) had helped her get 'the burnt stuff' into black plastic bags. Not everything from 'The Leap' was gone (only what had been on the table) and she was adamant she'd reconstruct what had been consumed by the fire from memory and push on, which was exactly what I would have expected. She felt 'lucky and quite stunned', she ended, and was now 'going to lie down'. And with that she signed off.

There had been troubling dispatches previously about burst pipes and broken boilers, lost keys and falling gutters, which were exactly the kinds of missives an aged parent might send a slightly less aged child – yet there'd never been one like this. But then her house had never previously caught fire because a candle had been left beside papers. Until this moment, according to her, house fires were the sort of misfortune that only happened to other people. But now the line had been crossed; now she was vulnerable to a new order of disaster to which she'd previously never been susceptible; now she was one of that cohort to whom this sort of tragedy might happen, a person whose house might burn down. On the edge of my thoughts, as this realisation trickled in, was Chekhov's *Peasants*, a novella she'd directed me to read as an adolescent, which includes a terrifying account of a fire in the Russian village of Zhukovo that destroys a house while the villagers look on hopelessly and only a student single-handedly tries and fails to put out the flames. The novella – with its pitiless account of the squalor of poverty-stricken Russian rural life at the end of the nineteenth century – is possibly, out of all of Chekhov's work, the bleakest (although *In the Ravine*, with its description of infanticide, might also claim that title) and coming to me at this moment it reinforced my own melancholy.

After I received the email and had read it, I called her immediately. I wanted assurances and I got them. Candles, she said, would never again be lit and left unattended. This did me no good. For days following the account of the fire, I was filled with the preternatural dread (registered as a feeling rather than a thought) that follows a near-death moment, say a car zipping past just as one is about to step off a kerb that brushes so close the displaced air, hot and smelling of petrol fumes, presses against the face like a hand. The feeling of terror lingered, entwined with the fretful feelings of powerlessness that come with living across the sea from where the old parent resides.

On the Wednesday following the fire, a brief email came from her which bore no traces of aftershock. Her recovery was quicker than mine. In this email the fire wasn't mentioned at all. As legendary as her capacity to turn experience into language was her capacity to move on. Instead in this email she noted, referring to the new Covid regulations, 'Life is very restricted and I doubt that it will ever ease up,' and then she continued, in reference to my having shown her how to use the dictation device on her iPhone: 'I am practising speaking the emails (but not this). People send them non-stop and they are getting very long and repetitive. Trying to work and eyes are not able to do much.'

As Covid rampaged and my apprehension of my mother's looming death deepened and hardened, my mind found it impossible to conceive of Covid as being the cause of her end. I found the idea unthinkable. It literally could not happen.

In the middle of May I delivered a novel, a retelling of the Oedipus story, *I, Antigone*. The very next day, I sat down and started *Tales We Tell Ourselves*. This was a selection of tales taken from Boccaccio's *The Decameron*, rewritten in demotic English. It was my publisher's idea. He believed modern readers living through a global pandemic might find Boccaccio's early Renaissance fiction, which was prompted and shaped by the Black Death, relevant. I hoped he was right but what attracted me to the project was less the present chiming with the past than a curious fact from Irish literary history. It was my understanding that James Joyce's first experience of Homer was Charles Lamb's *The Adventures of Ulysses* (1808). Who was to say what my retelling could catalyse in the same way Lamb's text had? On top of that, Boccaccio was a writer I loved and here was a way to introduce him to a new generation of readers.

For the rest of the month, I did nothing but eat, sleep and breathe *The Decameron*; I spoke to no one, and contacted no one. I just wrote and wrote and wrote. This obsessively singular, focused manner of writing was something I had seen my mother practise. Her work ethic in childhood had disappointed me because it had excluded me but it had also been instructive. By her example she had shown me that if a book had to be written, it could be. You just knuckled down and you didn't cavil or fret or regret imperfections. After all, infelicities could be amended later. The thing was to do it and to finish the damned thing and what I had been shown was possible I now managed myself as an adult. By the end of the month the draft was done and dispatched to my publisher.

*

Two days later, Thursday, 2 July 2020, I got this from my mother: 'Darling, I was working on Eliot and quoting this line: "Blown hair is sweet, brown hair over the mouth blown, lilac and brown hair." And I suddenly remembered the coral necklace you got me when you stayed with Mara and Lorenzo, and you were learning to play the flute. Thought it would please you to recall.' The email was short but the names, like iceberg tips poking up above the surface of the ocean, came with a huge bulk attached that was hidden below, the stuff of memory.

Lorenzo with his wife, Mara Berni, owned a restaurant in Beauchamp Place close to Harrods. It was called San Lorenzo. In the late 1960s my mother went there every week, usually taking my brother and me with her. Because of these regular visits, I came to know Mara and Lorenzo and one summer when the couple went on holiday to Forte dei Marmi (Lorenzo's home town) they brought me with them. I can't remember why. I have shadowy memories of endless delicious meals and interesting discoveries. I found out Lorenzo knew a great many anti-fascist partisans and communists and was left-leaning. In his restaurant in Beauchamp Place, he'd given no inkling of his political inclinations. In Italy I found myself wondering if Lorenzo had suppressed his political side when he was in his restaurant in London because his clientele mightn't have liked it. I never got an answer to that question but the experience was instructive. Human beings have extraordinary hidden hinterlands and they could be different people in different places.

At the holiday's end I felt I must buy my mother a really special present. I had money, which she'd given me, and I tramped the streets of Forte dei Marmi in search of something that would match my ambition. I was not an accomplished shopper. I spent days deliberating and weighing up my options before eventually I decided I would buy her a red coral necklace with a lovely clasp at the rear. The vendor wrapped my purchase in crisp sheets of tissue paper and put it in a box. This added to the gift's lustre. I believed only real jewellery was wrapped and boxed, or perhaps I thought its being wrapped and boxed proved it was real. I was certainly more excited by the wrapping and the box than by the necklace itself.

I presented the gift on my return. My mother told me I shouldn't have spent the money on her and I'd have been better spending it on myself. Whenever it came to money I'd been given, I was always told I could do with it whatever I wanted because it was my own. It's what she always said and I knew she meant it. At the same time, at the very moment I'd handed the necklace over and heard her out, I knew I'd been right to buy her something.

I'd assumed this moment of ancient history was forgotten – it was more than fifty years since I'd given her the coral necklace – and yet here, in her email, was proof it was not. In my mother's mind the object and the lines from Eliot connected. According to her account it was a case of involuntary memory: without conscious effort the Eliot line had prompted a recollection of a long-ago event. I wasn't so sure. I found myself wondering if her remembering wasn't a signal of her sense that death was drawing closer. Things which had to be said before their expression became impossible were drawing themselves to her attention and demanding they be expressed and this was one of them. Andrew Marvell's line from his poem 'To His Coy Mistress', where the poet hears 'Time's wingèd chariot hurrying near' was in my thinking here. My mother had heard the chariot's thrumming wheels getting louder and louder and that's what had provoked both her recall and her email. I couldn't know this of course, it was an assumption, but a mind on edge will do what it must to make sense of what it encounters.

In the summer my mother went away to the country with my brother and her grandson for a holiday and on Friday 17 July she wrote to tell me they'd had a beautiful day in a nature reserve in Kent and that now she was waiting for a taxi to take her back to London. She was working her way through her emails, she added, as she waited. I smiled as I read this. That was how she had always been; she had always had writing materials to hand, and whenever a few free minutes appeared, she'd draft whatever was pressing, sometimes a to-do list or a letter or a diary entry, sometimes a scene from a play or a film script or a story. This writing was always done pell-mell and always without any difficulty in switching between the practical and the creative. She could and did advance on many fronts at the same time. In my childhood she never went anywhere without one of the Challenge spiral notebooks she favoured then, and a couple of what she called 'good pens' (a good pen had to have a strong flow and produce a lovely rolling line) and as soon as a moment arose (sitting under the dryer in the hairdresser's, sitting in a taxi caught in traffic, sitting waiting at a table in a restaurant) the notebook would come out, and away she would go, scribbling frantically in her big looping handwriting. When I began to clock this, I assumed all writers were the same. Only when I got older did I understand that what was habitual practice for her wasn't habitual for everyone. Many writers, I came to realise, needed to be in a certain forcefield (a place, a mood, a state of mind) to write. If the circumstances weren't conducive, they couldn't access the internal space from where the work flowed. But my mother didn't need the conditions to be right to access her imagination (or for her imagination to access her). She could simply open the notebook, pull out the pen and within seconds, just like that, the words were tumbling forth, sometimes practical, sometimes creative, as first she dashed off the shopping list for the evening's dinner, and then five hundred words of a story.

Decades later she embraced new technology (the computer, the iPad, the iPhone) yet she never abandoned paper. In later years she still used spiral notebooks as well as yellow legal notepads, along with envelopes and other papery scraps that came to hand, for writing as much as for lists. Unchanged also was her indefatigability – did she refer to this as the Catholic work ethic? Or did I dream that? No, I think she did – and her ability to make use of any time in hand. So, as she waited for her taxi to come, she was tapping away at an email for me. Advancing on all fronts. Always.

Her email to me ended, 'So glad Boccaccio is done. What a relief. I am still with T. S. [Eliot] and sick of him.'

When I read this, it triggered a memory of something I'd learnt about the prolific Belgian novelist Simenon in Patrick Marnham's biography *The Man Who Wasn't Maigret: A Portrait of Georges Simenon*. I got my copy down from the shelf and found the reference I wanted. In 1960 Simenon was asked to give a radio talk on Balzac, and, as Marnham observes, 'It is an unexpected fact that this 7,000-word biographical essay took him one month to write, a period of time in which he was capable of writing three novels.'[2] I'd read the Marnham biography thirty years ago but this detail had stuck because it told a truth: if you're in the swing of it, fiction has a way of writing itself; if the gods are smiling, it happens, or it can happen (and my mother was the kind of writer to whom this happened, certainly in the early years) without effort, fluently. A lecture isn't like that. It takes time to read the sources, extract content and produce the copy; it is always work (although it can be happy work). Most importantly, unlike fiction, especially fiction which flows from personal experience – and everything my mother wrote, including the later political books, were drawn from what she knew – a lecture can't be created by an act of will. In my reply to my mother, I glossed the story of Simenon taking an age to draft his Balzac talk because I thought it would cheer her up to know he had suffered just as she was suffering with her own pursuit, the T. S. Eliot talk.

She wrote back immediately (still tapping away on her iPad of course): 'I must read that essay on Balzac. I admire Simenon very much. Faulkner praised him.' Her email continued, the tone light and very Colette-ish, 'the country air is a lot better than London' and because of the country air she was 'very drowsy' and 'would love to spend 4/5 nights

2 Patrick Marnham, *The Man Who Wasn't Maigret: A Portrait of Georges Simenon* (London: Bloomsbury, 1992), pp. 276–7.

[in the country] to get some energy back as it's in short supply'. Then came the line with the sting: 'Eliot has already taken me seven months and it's still in a heap.'

As the summer continued emails floated backwards and forwards across the Irish Sea. I tried to be encouraging, especially about the Eliot talk. In addition to emails there were phone calls, but the times had to be agreed and in the diary. Although she had always had a telephone and indeed loved the telephone and could talk away on it for hours, the telephone also made her nervous, or to be precise, the incoming calls the telephone facilitated made her nervous. She abhorred the way a call could come in and enable the caller to catch her unprepared. Her anxiety (it bordered on being a terror) was rooted in her need to always be in control.

And as she had got older her antipathy to the phone had got stronger. Of course, she would always answer it – there were emergencies, which meant the pesky thing had to be picked up – but what she really liked (at least with me) was to set a day and a time by email and then for me to ring at the agreed time, with no leeway tolerated. Five p.m. meant 5 p.m. not 4.55 p.m. or 5.05 p.m. In her opinion, punctuality was an indicator of moral character; people who rang when they said – they were people she could rely on and trust, whereas the rest (those who didn't ring when they were supposed to), they were scallywags, rogues and dissemblers. The terms of opprobrium were light but there was real judgement in play. When a person failed to call at the time agreed – or worse, failed to call altogether – they revealed they were riven by a deep and unforgivable flaw – an untrustworthiness which signalled a capacity for treachery – and once she had noticed this, she would be forever on her guard when with them.

In the case of my calls, the pattern that became established was that I would initiate the arrangement by email at the week's end and we would speak on Sunday evening at the precise time.

On the first Sunday of August I rang and she told me she couldn't speak but we would the next day. But then that Monday she wrote to say she felt 'very wobbly today' and therefore we couldn't talk. We'd have to postpone and 'talk later in the week'. By way of explaining her deferral she wrote, 'The work and the sicknesses are a bit much so I decided to just go to bed and try to get some strength back.'

And then this came in the evening: 'Darling I am sorry I had to be absent from the phone today but these sudden swerves into blackout frightened me and I had to lie down. It's all to do with blood trouble from the chemo and the dreaded shingles and T. S. Eliot. We will chat later in the week when I have been to two specialists.'

She continued that she hoped for relief and she hoped to resume working. An indefatigable Stakhanovite – from Stakhanov, the Soviet miner with the exemplary work ethic, the word, which we liked, was the gift of my father who picked it up in the 1930s at left-wing meetings – the idea of not working was unconscionable. Then she came to the final line of the email, whose charge was enhanced by its grammatical infelicitous-ness: 'I didn't ever imagine myself into illness but now I know it and how it alters everything in mind and memory.'

By the end of the week, she'd recovered. On Saturday, 8 August 2020 she wrote to say she'd been out in the garden of her house in Chelsea, writing and then, 'came in a little while ago to have something to eat as it began to get too dark to write outside. The day here has been so oppressive.' Rain was expected and waiting for the turn was like 'waiting for floodgates' to open. Her sensitivity to rain's imminence was perennial. Then she mentioned she had been chatting on the phone to the Northern Irish painter Colin Davidson, for whom she was going to sit for her portrait, and reported, 'he is a lovely person with a very truthful instinct, which matters so much. I'm hoping to see him in September.' I thought that was typical; she had too much to do and sitting would be exhausting yet she would do it, because it had to be done since that is what being in literature requires.

No career was possible without this level of commitment, which she had maintained all her life.

She ended the email with a flourish: 'Sending you love and hope that Old Boccaccio is in the bag.'

From my diary:

> Wednesday, 12 August 2020. I go for a walk and listen on my iPhone to a recording of the eighteenth-century English comic novel *The Life and Opinions of Tristram Shandy, Gentleman* (1759–1767) by Laurence Sterne. At one point I hear, 'And here I am sitting, this twelfth day of August, 1766, in a purple jerkin and yellow pair of slippers . . .'[3] Isn't today also August 12? I check my watch and delightedly I see, yes, it is. Synchronicity!

Sometime in the summer of 2020 I noticed a damp patch on one of the floorboards in the airing cupboard of the schoolhouse. The plumber came and carefully jemmied up the floorboard. Then he bent forward and shone his torch down.

'Ah ha,' I heard him exclaim. 'Here we are.'

Illuminated by the beam of his torch I saw a tiny needle of water spurting out of a pipe.

---

3 *The Life and Opinions of Tristram Shandy, Gentleman* by Laurence Sterne, Penguin English Library, Book Nine.

'Hold your breath,' said the plumber and I did and I heard the noise the water made as it shot out.

'Some force there,' said the plumber.

He took up more planks and revealed there was a pool of water under the house that stretched away in every direction, from one end of the building to the other.

'That's your mains feed,' he said pointing at the pipe with the tiny hole. 'I bet it's been leaking for years.'

I notified the insurers. A loss adjuster was appointed. A builder visited. He tested our pine floorboards and our stone walls for water content. The schoolhouse was saturated.

The builder outlined our future as follows:

1. Find somewhere else to live.
2. Put furniture in store.
3. Move out.
4. In the schoolhouse, rip up and cart away the pine floors, the joists and all wet timber. As there was rot, the materials would have to be disposed of carefully. A fortnight, maybe three weeks to do this.
5. Bring in half a dozen industrial dehumidifiers. To dry the schoolhouse out would take five weeks minimum.
6. Lay new foundations, new joists, insulating membrane. A fortnight.
7. Lay a new wooden floor. Another fortnight.
8. Repaint the whole house inside. Weeks . . .

At the end of the conversation, we added up the days.

Total length of time required, four months minimum, more like five or six, but best to allow seven or eight. And worse-case scenario (say if something hideous showed up that hadn't been anticipated) it could be a year. A year! We would be out of our home for a year.

At the end of August my mother wrote to me: she had heard from a mutual friend about the leak and that we would have to leave our house: 'ye have to move out due to a leak?' her email began. 'I will call this evening about 6 if that's okay. I also have to move out: whole house [has to be] rewired, floors dug up, etc. and CHAOS plus mega expense.' She would have to pay, she explained, as the landlord had insisted the dilapidations were down to her. 'Life is not a cruise,' she ended. Kinship through catastrophism, I thought. I knew this well. She had often matched misery with misery, I had noticed, hers to other people's and vice versa. It had always been a brilliant means of forging connection.

Being the admirer of coincidence that I am, I thought: first there was the *Tristram Shandy* correlation of dates and now there's the correspondence of both of us having to move out; what'll be the third connection? My pattern-finding brain was incorrigible.

Later I began to have other thoughts about her moving out to facilitate the rewiring of her house and back to me came the phrase from her email, 'mega expense'. It was so light and insouciant, though I knew it masked profound anxiety about money. Yes, she had made money since she began publishing in the 1960s. She had also spent it. Recklessly, improvidently, though latterly her extravagance was tempered. It had to be. She couldn't spend like she had because she had not made proper provision for her old age. She had few assets. Of course, had she taken the orthodox home-ownership route she would now be living rent-free but she wasn't built to do things the orthodox way and as she was about to enter her ninth decade she was living in a rented house, as she had been since the 1980s. She was still working, of course, and still earning. She made money, some money but never as much as she would have wished. Publishing, as she had often complained, was not what it had been. Smaller advances. More required of the poor old author. More emphasis on marketing and media. And beyond publishing, a less favourable cultural ecosystem. And in the world at large, more philistinism. Often, she speculated ludically on the desirability and even necessity of her having a patron. Talking of this fabled figure was a way of acknowledging, slantwise, the problem. There had been money, there was still some money but there wasn't enough. For a working writer, a successful working writer, everything had got harder, though, as she hinted, help was afforded by friends, usually in kind, though again this was never discussed. As always, the country-woman's absolute discretion.

On Saturday 5 September my mother wrote to me. It was a long letter, reminiscent of those I used to receive from her when I was at boarding school, light and funny and full of gossip and family lore. It was full of work as well. 'On with Eliot and tasks galore,' she observed. At the end she mentioned she had done something by video at Trinity College in Dublin (a translation-related talk) and she had used Walter Benjamin and Samuel Johnson in her talk as I had suggested, and for this she thanked me. Wow, I thought when I finished. Her form was good; her mood was optimistic. After a long and difficult climb could I hope the plateau had been reached? It turned out it had. A month later, on Saturday 3 October, I received a long, happy email from her. She was in the country, which was a 'miracle' on account of her being able to work without interruption at a long table. The house (she didn't say where it was) was 'very luxurious'; she was enjoying 'beautiful dinners' but best of all was the 'underfloor heating', which was 'wonderful'.

Her words about the underfloor heating shot me straight back to childhood. To keep us warm in our house in Morden, 257 Cannon Hill Lane, we burnt lustrous, semi-metallic-seeming chunks of anthracite, which were hard to light in the open fire in the dining room at the back of the house, and the stove in my father's study at the front from which hot water was pumped to the single radiator in the clothes press in the hall. There was also a tiny stove in the kitchen but its flue leaked smoke and it was rarely lit. There were gas fires in the bedrooms but they were only turned on for a few minutes before bed. My father believed they were a fire hazard. The brick-built house with its linoleum floors was chilly, especially in the long London winters, and my mother, who believed she'd inherited her mother's poor circulation, was always cold, and because of this, throughout my childhood, she would regularly hold out her fingers and say, 'Go on, feel my fingers. Feel how cold I am.'

I always held her fingers as instructed but never attempted to judge their temperature. I just agreed that they were cold, which thrilled her. It was always a victory when her genetic inheritance was confirmed. Until prompted by her email I hadn't thought about this for decades but knowing her susceptibility to the cold was lifelong I recognised what a boon the underfloor heating, wherever she was, must be.

The plateau period continued. My worries receded. I became complacent.

But all good things end. On Sunday, 18 October 2020, she wrote to tell me the joys of being in the luxurious house in the country, being warm and eating well, were now a thing of the past. She was back in her house in Ovington Street, 'very tired and depleted after working all day. Still on this Eliot lecture and have tied myself up in knots.' She didn't want to be telephoned; that would have to wait until the following weekend and rather than my ringing her, she'd ring me. I knew that was her way of saying she mightn't be able to speak to me because she was too frazzled, or too exhausted, or too enervated by her struggle to write, and she was preparing me for that. Because she was the one who'd call rather than me and the caller had the right to cancel, she was entitled to send an email cancelling whatever arrangement had been arrived at just before it was supposed to happen. This was a further refinement of our telephone protocol. She ended, 'I hope things are well though life is gloom on all fronts. Just pray that Trump loses and loses big time . . . We have to keep faith and hope and yes, charity.' Here was another characteristic. Her interest in politics and recoil from the enemies of progress never receded no matter what was happening in the rest of her life. In fact, her political antagonisms, if anything, got fiercer as she aged. She really seemed to fear for the world.

On Sunday 25 October my mother was meant to phone at 6.30 p.m. but having forgotten the clocks went back an hour that morning she rang at the time she would have called if the clocks hadn't changed, which was 7.30 p.m., an hour later. Her voice was not her old voice, the one I'd been hearing all my life. What I heard was similar, but less musical, thinner, more careworn, tremulous and a tiny bit bewildered. I had been rattled by the fire and what it signified but this was worse. It was a shock to realise that what had never not been heard for the decades I had lived I would now never hear again. Her voice was one of the most important components of her Edna-ness. But now it had vanished. An extinction moment.

In her new voice she explained again that her landlord was insisting she move out while her house was rewired. A neighbour, she explained, had found a lawyer to fight the landlord pro bono.

As I listened, I rationalised: the nightmare of being unhomed, albeit temporarily, was what was causing her to speak in the new reduced way I was hearing. The loss of her voice was the physical cost of her looming expulsion.

The call finished. I didn't move out of my chair in the living room where I was sitting. Habitually, I deflect by rushing about and while I'm whirling around, the misery trickles away, but this moment was too big for that kind of remedy. There was nothing else for it but to honour my apprehension of what I knew was coming on account of the change in her voice. So, I sat and thought about my mother's dying and as I sat it grew dark outside the huge schoolhouse windows. At some point (it was quite dark by now), I heard my phone ping. That would be an email from my mother, I predicted. A sad encounter was always followed – and quickly at that – by a message which would attempt to quell any anxieties that might be lingering and assert her indomitability, her determination to keep on keeping on. I opened the phone. It was as I thought. I wasn't surprised. This was part of the protocol too.

She was sorry, she wrote, for how she'd been on the phone. Everything was awry for her. There was the matter of the clock change, which was confusing and disorientating, and on top of that it had been a day of 'odd interruptions': a doctor had paid a house call and 'stayed one hour, when I was trying to get back to work'. I knew that would have maddened her. She had so little time left and any time she got she wanted to devote to her Eliot lecture. Then she riffed about the lawyer her neighbour had found. She wasn't hopeful this remedy would work. She ended gloomily, speaking of the landlord, 'I fear they will behave like bullies.'

She rounded off as follows: 'Just now I watched the end of the news and it said that four years ago Hillary Clinton was the same number of points ahead of Trump as Joe Biden now is, and still Trump swung it. A terrifying prospect. We will talk soon and I won't get time wrong. I am about to have a drink.'

I couldn't pretend I hadn't heard the voice I'd heard but these sentences heartened me. She was still engaged with the world. She was still raging against the monsters. She was still taking a drink.

My wife and I had originally moved from London to County Fermanagh in 1989 so that I could research a book about what were wrongly termed the Troubles and which was actually a civil war; this book was eventually published under the title, *The Glass Curtain: Inside an Ulster Community*. The plan had always been that we would return to London with the children once the book was finished but we didn't do that. Instead, two years after we'd arrived, we bought an old 1930s Lutyens-style school outside Enniskillen, with two classrooms, two cloak rooms, a kitchen, and separate entrances for boys and girls. Twenty-nine years later, my wife and I (mostly my wife) spent the last week of October 2020 getting the schoolhouse ready for the builders, who were coming in to sort out the problems caused by the leak. Everything small was boxed and stored in the attic. The big pieces were removed on the morning of the last Saturday of the month and carried away to the local furniture depository. Once the schoolhouse rooms were empty, we walked around and remembered we'd last seen them like this when we arrived here in August 1991.

Then we locked up and left the keys in the shed for the builder who was starting on Monday and drove four miles to the house where we'd be living until the work at the schoolhouse was finished.

Our new home was on the edge of an Irish wood at the entrance to an old estate. Once upon a time there must have been a gate lodge here; a small classic building, two or three rooms only, with a slate roof and tiny windows, in which lived a whole family whose job was to open and close the demesne gates for every carriage that appeared. In my imagination the gate lodge had Gothic windows and a crooked front door and the inhabitants had stepped straight out of Maria Edgeworth's *Castle Rackrent*. But the old gates were gone – there was just an open entrance (gates were no longer required to keep out the mutinous peasantry it seemed) – and the old gate lodge was gone too, and on the site where it once stood there was a bungalow built in the second half of the twentieth century with a car porch tacked to the back. This would be our new home for the winter, at least, probably the spring, maybe even the summer.

It was a Sunday morning when I woke up in the gate lodge that was not a gate lodge after my first night there. I drew the curtains and looked out; I saw trees and the banks of a stream that cut through the surrounding woods and I heard pigeons cooing, that lovely, soft, balmy sound. I went to the kitchen and made coffee (I hadn't acclimatised to the new order so this took an age) and then I opened my computer.

There was an email from my mother, the first I received in my new temporary home. She was always good at being first. She began by wishing me 'Good luck' in my 'new abode'. Then she wondered if I'd had to move all my books and papers. It was a heartfelt enquiry; at the same time, it was personal.

She had always been an indefatigable reviser with a liking for peripatetic practice. She liked to have different workstations dotted around, in the kitchen, in the dining room, in the sitting room, and to move between them, sieving and revising her words until she judged the time was right and all the papers from all the different workstations could be brought together and welded into a glorious whole. It was an odd and unwieldy system but owing to her exacting memory – she could always lay her hand on whatever she wanted wherever it was – it worked for her. But it only worked if her papers remained undisturbed until the time came to gather them in with the other papers and fashion a master document. If papers had to be moved before they were ready – disaster.

Her question about my having to move my books and papers therefore sprung from her apprehension that if her house had to be rewired and she was forced to move out (this matter was apparently not totally settled yet, although I had thought it had been) this might be her fate. But this was no surprise; it's so often what worries us that we worry about on everyone else's behalf. Our cares for the other spring from our own terror. As it happens, my working pattern was diametrically the opposite of hers: I don't like working in different places and having different sections of work in different places waiting for agglomeration. And yes, I had had to move books and papers when we left the schoolhouse and moved to the new house but, in my case, I'd moved them from one desk to another, the very desk (actually a table) where I was sitting reading her email.

In her email's middle, lodged like a splinter, lay another of her anxieties, one with which I was also familiar. 'A new girl,' she wrote, 'is coming to type in a few minutes' which in turn meant our telephone call would have to wait. In order that I should better understand, she added: 'Dreading her arrival. But I need someone desperately.'

After I read this, a sense of déjà vu. When we lived in Morden she typed everything herself. But when she moved to Putney after she and my father parted, she had to write more as she became more successful. Now, as well as stories and novels, she was writing theatre and play scripts, reviews and occasional articles. And then there was her correspondence. There were several posts each day in the 1960s in London; the postman brought bundles of post with each delivery and these in turn must be answered. On the hall table in the Putney houses and later in the Chelsea house, I would regularly see piles of ten or twenty letters waiting to be carted to the box. To manage assistance was necessary and it came in the form of a succession of secretaries who came many times in the week and spent hours closeted with my mother in her study, either typing up what she'd written in her spiral notebooks or taking dictation and addressing envelopes and parcels. They would also answer the phone, transcribe messages, run to the post office, go to the shops and ferry clothes to and from the dry cleaners. My mother paid well but her standards were exacting and meticulous and her manner was pitiless. Her relationships with those who came to help were sometimes fraught. Sometimes she was the agent of her own difficulties and sometimes she was not and things were not in her control. These women became huge figures in her life (how could they not when they were helping her so much and in the house for so long and so often?). Without fail every one became an inexhaustible talking point, for she talked and indeed brooded endlessly about those who helped her and the idea of the ideal helper – a figure who was always there, almost within reach but who always, at the last moment, somehow slipped away.

In old age she still needed secretarial help despite the replacement of the typewriter by the iPad and the personal computer. Her relationships remained complex, and psychological fundamentals never changing, her torments when a new helper was anticipated (as per her email) were bound to be the same as those which had scorched her in the 1960s. Would they work well together, she and this as yet unknown helper? Or would they not?

And it was not just simple personal compatibility that was the issue at stake, although that's what it often came down to. As she had always seen it and still saw it, the real issue was the work and its survival at the moment of its emerging from her unconscious before it got onto the page. When she worked with someone, she either read from handwritten sheets, changing what she had written as she read, or made it up on the spot without the aid of notes. She could dictate off the cuff and when she did her voice had a strange, tranced, otherworldly quality. It was easy to fancy overhearing her like this that the Sibyls sounded a bit like this when Apollo spoke through them.

If she and whomever was working for her, tapping away at the typewriter or later, the iPad or the iMac, clicked (which had to do both with their behaviour before they began work and the precision and speed with which they carried off the business of producing clean copy) everything went swimmingly and the flow was effortless. That was the ideal, something to yearn for. But if the relationship went wrong, the words couldn't happen and that entailed more than a temporary loss. If the words hadn't a safe passage at birth because she and her helper were in conflict, they would miscarry and be lost forever. I knew that was what underpinned her words, 'Dreading her arrival. But I need someone desperately.' It was permanent loss she feared. This was something we had often discussed. Quoting Hemingway, who advised stopping at whatever one's typical daily word count was, 800 words say, even in mid-sentence because, as he promised, the mind would complete the sentence on one's return to the page, I argued the unconscious never lost anything, ever. It always gave. The words were never lost. They were always given. But she did not believe me.

At the end of the email, she alluded to her woes with her house. 'Battles with landlord.' And then she concluded: 'All a bit upside down and now lockdown.' It was all too much for her, the present.

On the Monday, close to when we were meant to talk, she deferred again. 'May I say tomorrow at 6.30?' she wrote. Her day, she explained, 'has been one of complete agitation'. Neighbours were excavating a basement and the digging machinery had started thumping at 5 a.m. She spent 'all day' (probably an exaggeration but I know how she felt) on the phone to the council speaking to someone she referred to as 'a noise abatement person'. Always the sly wit, I thought, reading that. She wasn't impressed by whomever she spoke to (which was hardly surprising). 'They all lie and dissimulate.' She was sorry to 'mess' me around but she was simply too harassed to talk. 'Life should be a bit easier at 90,' she ended, 'and instead it's far more difficult. I will feel a bit calmer tomorrow.' The ruefulness was familiar but not any less chastening for being so. At the end of life, it ought not to be what she was reporting. But amelioration seemed unlikely. Here was a truth to anneal one's pessimism, mine certainly.

Our communications over November were fitful. We spoke, probably on Saturdays, but I didn't record any details in my diary. On the final Friday of November, she wrote to say, 'I would normally ring tomorrow but Eliot' – her lecture on T. S. Eliot – had to be recorded on the first Friday in December, the fourth, and she was 'in a heap, hence panic!! I will call next weekend.' Her birthday was looming (15 December, the lecture would be streamed that day) and she had written to my wife, she said, to say no presents were to be sent. 'I don't want anything,' she wrote, 'just to hang on that bit longer.'

On the last day of 2020 she wrote this: 'Darling. Had the vaccine.' I knew by this point how frightened she was of the Covid-19 virus. The idea of contagion and death by respiratory failure in a hospital, like the people she'd seen on the television, surrounded by staff in gowns and visors, appalled her. Death was never welcome but this version – excruciating, lonely and solitary – she particularly reviled. That she could write about her inoculation was for her, I knew, a colossal relief. Yet despite this, and what an achievement it was to get the shot so early, her email's tone was elegiac, mournful. 'It was lovely to be out,' she wrote, speaking of her trip to the inoculation centre, 'but London seems sad and worn-out. I saw only three taxis in all.' As a non-driver who depended totally on taxis for most of her life to get around London and elsewhere, taxi numbers were a subject of perennial interest and another subject about which, as I remember from childhood, she never tired of talking. That there were now only three taxis to be seen in all the great city of London was, I didn't doubt for her, given her London-cab obsession, the surest sign that the pandemic had turned the world upside down.

At the end of the email came one of her characteristic turns where she asserted her determination to keep on keeping on, despite everything, ageing, the pandemic, the state of the world. Yes, she conceded, because of the injection she'd received and the old year's end and the memories the occasion inevitably stirred up, she would be 'a wee bit mopey' on New Year's Eve itself, but this would be temporary; as far as 2021 was concerned, she had plans in place. Now the lecture on T. S. Eliot was done and dusted, she was moving on to her play *Joyce's Women* and she would work on the script on New Year's Day. 'Work is a great companion,' she explained, 'despite its anxieties.' A very telling sentence. Composition was no exception to the roster of anxiety-provoking activities but in the hierarchy, it was far less troubling than so many other things. 'We are lucky in so many ways.' I cut and pasted this email into my journal (as I did with everything) but underneath I added a comment. 'If I want to know the origin of my Stakhanovite (or workaholic) tendencies, I need look no further than my mother.'

2021

Two days into the new year she wrote: 'It's freezing in this house.'

The house to which she was referring was a rackety, three-storey, utterly idiosyncratic Georgian or early Regency building, which she had filled with beautiful things and made into a lovely place to be. She'd always been good at that sort of thing.

The first house she owned was 9 Deodar Road in Putney, a three-bedroom terraced house of yellowy London brick. When she bought it in the early sixties (I'm not sure of the year, 1965 or 1966 perhaps) she hadn't made much money and she couldn't afford new furniture from a department store or classic pieces (which she'd have liked) from antique shops. Instead, she bought everything she needed at a small auction house on the nearby Lower Richmond Road, to which she could walk. She went every week and every week something came home with her from there, usually in a taxi. One Saturday morning, there being a sale on, and having got 'dolled up' (crucial, she explained, if she was to succeed, though I didn't understand why this was) she took me with her.

The sales room smelt of damp and the Thames, which was nearby, and stewed tea. It was filled with furniture, books and household items, all of which appeared, at first glance, shabby and dirty and unwanted. I only realised much later that this was where the flotsam and the jetsam of London's working and lower-middle classes washed up when their houses were cleared after they died. A lot of what was for sale wasn't to my mother's taste but there were gems to be found here and there – providing your eye was good and hers was – and she found them and she didn't have to pay very much for them either.

My mother got the list of what was for auction – a set of mimeographed sheets stapled together – and marched around incredibly quickly, circling in Biro on her sheets the lot numbers (grubby tickets, obviously recycled from week to week) of the things which she wished to bid on. Her decision-making process was quick, brisk and certain. The same was true of her bidding once that was underway. It was obvious as I stood beside her, watching her hand go up and down, that the other bidders (mostly stall-holders or small antique or bric-a-brac shop owners) knew her by sight and even reputation, not as a writer of course but as a bidder, a collector, a buyer and a ruthless competitor. I didn't quite follow how the process went and lots were secured but at the end of the sale I found she had acquired, along with jugs, plates and glasses, a black papier-mâché table inlaid with mother-of-pearl and a matching chair.

We carried the furniture out to the Lower Richmond Road along with a cardboard box with the other things inside wrapped in old newspaper. She set the table and chair on the kerb and I put the box on the table, and she started to look for a taxi. Eventually one appeared, heading for Putney High Street. She flagged it down. 'Deodar Road,' she said. The driver shook his head. He was heading for Fulham and the West End (a left at Putney High Street and straight over Putney Bridge) and he didn't want to take a short fare (a right at the High Street and then left along the Wandsworth Bridge Road and on a few hundred yards to Deodar Road). But my mother would not take his no. She pressed, she flattered, she appealed, she cajoled. She promised a tip. And eventually she prevailed, just like she did with every driver every time.

A few minutes later we alighted at number 9 Deodar Road and carried in the purchases. There followed the rearranging process by which the new was integrated with the old. The furniture that was already there was moved around and the black papier-mâché table and chair inserted, first here then there, until a new harmony was established. It was the same with the plates and jugs and glasses. These were tried on shelves and in cupboards before a resting place was decided. It was a fiendish and finagling process but when everything had been settled, I looked around and realised (in the manner of an eleven- or twelve-year-old) that my mother had a talent for this.

Over the following decades this capacity got stronger (helped by having money) and her last house, the Ovington Street house, was probably the best put together of all the houses whose interiors and gardens she curated.

Sadly, her capacity for making a place beautiful was not matched by an interest in modern domestic technology. Her Chelsea house, which she rented and where she lived for longer than anywhere else in her life, well over thirty and nearing forty years, was last refurbished, at a guess, in the twentieth century. As the years rolled on her neighbours installed triple glazing and underfloor heating and made their houses snug and cosy. Her home, however, remained the house she'd taken in the mid-1980s. She had therefore put it precisely. 'It's freezing in this house.' It was. And as a person who felt the cold, this was a particular ordeal.

The rest of the email was about work. Eliot was behind her and she had moved on (without breaking stride) to *Joyce's Women*. It was going to be hard ('challenging') fashioning a drama from this material, but it would be easier than the Eliot lecture. Her unconscious was always happiest inventing as opposed to critiquing or analysing. All she had to do was to ask it to make her something and it would and it didn't matter if it was drama or prose. The unconscious always obliged. That was part of her creative capacity.

In January, I was preoccupied by what had happened on 6 January in Washington DC on Capitol Hill, and by the pandemic and by the student scripts I had to mark and the infernal list of cares arising from the works ongoing at the schoolhouse to rectify the damage caused by flooding. At some point I confessed that it was all too much and on Tuesday 19 January my mother wrote to me about this. She sympathised. Covid 'had made everyone fearful' and weary. 'Life is not natural for anyone just now' she noted, for herself along with everyone else. She had been scheduled to have her second vaccine in two days but this, she had heard just before she wrote to me, had been cancelled. As a result, she was in 'a state'. Of course, she didn't want to die the Covid way, which she understood was like drowning. As a non-swimmer who was frightened of water all her life, the notion of a Covid death as being like drowning was terrifying. She also didn't want to die, full stop, because she had work to do, the play and no doubt other things I didn't know about. Not to achieve, not to finish, not to complete, would be an affront to one of her most cherished personal beliefs. Writers or artists who just talked the talk but didn't 'produce the goods', as she liked to put it, had always offended her. She only had time and respect for those who got the thing written and out into the world, exactly as she had done all her life.

For this reason, the idea that she would not give expression in language to what she had within and knew was waiting to be translated into language because the virus had killed her before she could do the work was a contemptible idea and she was just not having it. 'Work and worries abound,' she concluded, but 'we have to just plough on and hope, hope for ourselves and for others.' And then, at the end, the characteristic turn, as so often in her emails, to the political and the wayward ways of the world. 'Meanwhile, gun sales in America are escalating,' she wrote. 'Just try and have faith in yourself and your aspirations. It will all improve but this is a very testing time.' What I took as her message was this: it wasn't just a question of maintaining a proper relationship with the unconscious, which was what every artist must manage; it was also a question of dealing with the insanity flooding in from without that threatened to unbalance the mind and mess up the relationship with the unconscious. To face in two directions, outwards and inwards, and to fight on both fronts simultaneously – that was the task.

It was decreed. Her house in Chelsea must be rewired and she must leave. A friend offered sanctuary in a flat in central London and my mother moved there. At the end of March, she wrote to apologise for not being in touch; moving 'was a bit of strain'. The new domicile was 'easier to write in' than her 'jumbled house' and she was 'lucky to be given this chance while rewiring is going on' but it was 'lonely'; though 'that's everywhere' she added, perhaps seeking to minimise the loneliness by making it universal. Well, it might be but this was still a jolt. Lonely! Her social life, so I had always thought, was rich and varied. Was I wrong? Yes. Here was a rebuke for having assumed what I had assumed rather than taking the trouble to find out. Perhaps I hadn't taken the trouble, it now occurred to me, because I feared turning something up I mightn't like, something like this.

Lurking at the email's end, a final line, which compounded the idea of loneliness. In the new flat, she wrote, the 'technology . . . [was] . . . daunting' and wouldn't work. Technology meant, I knew, for her, the television and the Sky box. With age she'd become an avid consumer of news (the Channel 4 news especially) and football. She followed no one team but preferred what she called 'the best games', rhapsodised endlessly about moments of excellence on the pitch and could be elevated in terms of mood by really good play: football did wonders for her. Many times, when I rang, if it wasn't Krishnan Guru-Murthy or Matt Frei that I heard in the background, it was the unmistakable roar of the supporters at whatever match she was watching, and after opening pleasantries she would always have to put down the phone and find the remote and reduce the sound. News and football really were a companion. And to have to forgo them because she couldn't get the telly to work was daunting. Daunting.

She signed off, 'Two or maybe three more weeks they reckon.' She meant till she could go back home. 'Cost will be considerable.' Of course, I thought. 'I hope you are well and not too daunted by Zooms and all else.' Daunted again. Because of its dual appearance I was prompted to look it up and check its meaning. The example cited of the word in use was, 'some people are daunted by technology'. Another coincidence, I thought, for my list.

At Easter she sent greetings. The rewiring wasn't done. It would be a fortnight before she got back to her jumbled house. She was busy: 'Working away on Joyce but it's quite lonely here, as I don't know any neighbours.' The jolt again, like the last time I'd seen the 'L' word and then a couple of sentences later, another shock: 'this pandemic has made . . . most of the world nuts and scams now are so numerous and so deceptive'. Her friend S, she went on to explain, just the evening before, had been visiting (the regulations were loosening) and had saved her when someone telephoned purporting to be from her bank and tried to persuade her to give them a lot of her money. As usual, she didn't do either self-pity or explanation when she gave her account; she just testified to the facts and moved on.

The venal preying on the old and solitary was not news to me. I had worked in prisons, for decades. I had taught prisoners who swindled (and worse) the old. I didn't like it but from these men I had always managed, I think, to keep my feelings hidden as I knew these would have driven them off. I believed it was paramount to keep teaching because I knew it was education that transformed attitudes and enabled culpability to be admitted freely – something judgement, and for that matter punishment, never managed. But after reading this email my fidelity to what I liked to think of as my professional standards vanished. All I could think of the scammer who'd tried to talk my mother into giving her card details was this: how could you prey on an old lady? You should be ashamed of yourself. When it's personal, reason vanishes and is replaced with ancient, more vengeful attitudes.

Some years ago, the American biographer Cathy Curtis contacted me. She was writing my mother's biography, unauthorised. Would I be able to put her and my mother in touch? she asked. I went to my mother with the request and the answer that came back was 'No.' Now Cathy Curtis was in touch again. She mightn't have been able to talk to my mother but could she talk to me in connection with her biography?

I didn't want to say 'no' without first consulting my mother. Perhaps she might approve, I thought. Perhaps. Well, probably not but still I had to ask. So, on a warm and sunny Saturday I dictated the following on my iPhone: 'I am out walking the lanes. The morning is quiet and damp and a bit misty. The cow parsley is out. Hawthorn in bloom. The cows sitting in the fields are like monumental sculptures. It's very quiet. I've been contacted by a woman called Cathy Curtis. She told me that she is writing your biography[4] but it's unauthorised and she wants to talk to me. She is in America. What would you like me to do?'

Her reply was swift. 'My agent is writing to her to say it is not possible. She wrote last year posing as a friend of yours. She is trying it on.' Moreover, my mother continued, 'we have appointed an official biographer who will have access to my papers, etc. and whom I have chosen'. A biography by an official biographer was in train: no purpose would be served by my speaking to an unofficial biographer. That was on the surface of her email. But below there was exasperation, even fury. This had two sources.

4 Cathy Curtis, *Fearless: A Biography of Edna O'Brien* (New York: Atmosphere Press, 2025).

On the one hand, history. In return for fame an individual pays a very high price in terms of loss of privacy and she had paid heavily over time. Over the course of her long life many had come to her door asking for this or that because she was famous; Curtis, as she saw it, just being the latest, and she was done with all that.

And on the other, her circumstances. Her eyes were 'wretched' and 'the chaos since I got back is a lot: nothing but boxes and bags and bits of Joyce in various envelopes. I feel I can't clear it and can't find lamps, plugs, the daily needs. But today and tomorrow I have enlisted help. The wiring, etc. cost me a fortune and I just hope your insurers coughed up. Wordsworth was right, "we lay waste our powers".'[5] Acutely aware of finitude, she was more anxious than ever to husband what time she had left and she couldn't take any harrying whatsoever.

A few hours later she wrote again. It was a pattern; the melancholy communication quickly followed by its antidote. This follow-up – motivated by her ancient determination to have all terms agreed in advance – concerned our imminent visit to London in July to see her. It was brisk and business-like. The will to control seemingly unassuageable.

5 'Getting and spending, we lay waste our powers,' from William Wordsworth's sonnet, 'The World Is Too Much with Us' (1807).

One, she regretted she couldn't see us in the afternoon of the day we arrived in London: 'sorry about that but [I have] an earlier appointment that I can't change'.

Two, we were to bring absolutely nothing. ('Please don't bring drink or food' – she always said this and we always blithely ignored this instruction.)

Three, she was sorry she couldn't see the children (it was just my wife and I who'd visit) but the chemo she'd received 'being too drastic' for her she could no longer 'do too much or see too many people'; however, she'd see the children separately, she assured me, once she got 'a bit of strength back'.

Four, she was looking forward to our visit. ('We will have a calm and happy time.')

She ended with an update of the usual kind, which mixed the assertion that she was working with an admission of the physical toll it was costing: 'Trying to get Joyce into theatrical shape and may not succeed . . . Eyes not able to carry on as I worked 5/6 hours and feel dizzy.'

In mid-June (Tuesday 15 June, to be precise) there was what she called a 'drama'. It concerned foxes. Some years earlier foxes had settled in her garden and made an earth or den. The vixen or vixens had birthed kits. Her garden was small and the adults and their young, so close to her house, oppressed her with their mess and their noise. But the kits grew to adulthood, the earth's entrance was sealed and that, as far as I understood, was the fox saga over. But now I understood it wasn't. The foxes were back. They had got into the basement and the previous Friday she'd sighted one in what she called the 'passage' and thought she had chased it out: but she hadn't; it was back in the basement. She got a neighbour in. He chased it away but what she 'didn't know was there was another fox' in the basement. This animal 'hurled [itself] against walls all night' and when she got another man in on Saturday 'the room was all blood, faeces, books eaten, things broken'. This second fox was now gone too. It had got out to the back porch, 'smashed everything' and, which was still a mystery, somehow escaped. That was Saturday and that should have been the end of everything. But it wasn't. There was still a last straw, as there always is. Nina, who came Sundays to help, went down to the basement to clean up. She was hoovering when, from under a cushion, a newborn kit emerged. My mother closed the email with a mix of insouciance and confession: 'things have been awry' she wrote and then, 'I was totally terrified and still very jumpy. Looking forward to seeing you both on July 2nd. Work very stalled and health not too good.'

I wrote immediately. What happened with the kit? I asked.

'It actually made its way out when Nina turned on the hoover,' she replied. 'I am still in shock. Fear more are hiding.'

I established that the basement had been checked and no more foxes were lurking and that the porch had been sealed so none could get back in. She confirmed all had been done but I wasn't reassured. The first thing I would do I knew when we got to her house for our visit at the start of July was check the basement.

And when we arrived, it was exactly so. I said a quick 'Hello' and bolted down to the basement. I checked the rooms (empty) and the porch door (locked and reinforced with plywood board).

A few minutes later I was back in the kitchen. My mother was in her preferred chair, the throne-like one with the good back support the other chairs didn't have and which, with age, she'd come to rely on more and more. She looked etiolated and insubstantial, but at the same time she was lucid and clear.

The fox 'drama' was still much on my mind and though I knew I shouldn't (what good would it do?) I couldn't not ask about it.

'Where did you see the fox?'

'Here in the house you mean?' she said.

'Yes.'

I'd assumed she'd seen it in the basement. I'd assumed she'd heard something and gone down to see. She'd said 'passage' in her email and so I'd assumed she'd meant the corridor in the basement.

'That's where I saw the fox,' she said.

She pointed through the kitchen door and into the tiny front hall on the other side of which was the front door through which I'd just come in.

'I got an awful fright,' she said.

I was wrong to assume as I had, which I did because it made the situation more comfortable, that she'd seen the animal in the basement, which was separate (at least in my mind) from the upper storeys where she lived. What happened was she'd been here, sitting exactly where she was sitting now, probably with a glass of white wine when, just a couple of feet away, she'd seen the animal pass. Her terror must have been incredible with my own lagging not far behind. This revelation triggered a tsunami of anxiety. I left the kitchen, returned to the back porch, found more sheets of plywood and wedged these behind every spot which was already reinforced.

We left my mother and went to an outdoor bar where we met three of our children. On the giant screens the Italy–Belgium UEFA EURO 2020 match (held over because of Covid) was showing and the space was full of Italian supporters. The crowds were exuberant and their cries full-throated and joyful; it ought by rights to have been easy to lose myself in the moment but I couldn't. All I could think about were the foxes.

*

Wednesday 21 July. My dream: I am in a train station: humming rails (the rails are humming in the heat), standing carriages, empty platforms. It might be King's Cross Station, it might be Heuston Station in Dublin. In the distance, I see my mother who is also not my mother, very lanky and gaunt-looking, wearing a long dress (almost nineteenth century) walking (gliding) along beside a brick wall. (There are shunting yards on the other side.) The figure's shoulders are rounded and she is looking down at the ground as she walks and I know the figure – my mother and not my mother – is walking towards death. I am filled with sadness and despair and grief.

I woke and wrote to her immediately. After such a dream, how could I not? I wanted to know she was still alive. She replied instantly. She was away, accompanied by London-based Irish property developer Paddy McKillen who she explained, 'brought me in his plane to Provence for a few days and it IS total luxury BUT I fainted in the heat today. I was doing my utmost to make progress with Joyce but fear it won't happen here. All the blood and cancer problems and shingles got worse so had to lie down. This old age is cruel and unpredictable.'

Like her mother before her, she was all omertà when it came to her health. Her health was not discussed except in the sketchiest terms in the bulletins and whenever I had tried to get her to talk (and I had certainly tried over the preceding months and years, as I had known she was ill) she had always closed the conversation down, ruthlessly. But now there was this small admission, the longest to date I'd received; it wasn't much but it seemed significant, particularly as it came with the tag, 'This old age is cruel and predictable.' There was a line. She was trapped in the room with no door. There was no escape from finiteness.

If she hadn't 'this play hanging over me I would just lie down and let the air drift over me', she continued, which sounded a new note of exhaustion, previously unheard. I also didn't quite believe it. Going by experience, fatigue would be overcome. If she did lie down, she would not stay down. She would get up and push on. She always did.

Her sign-off was a zinger: 'The poor beleaguered world is zany.' A perfect line for Poor Tom (it has his tender clarity) in a gritty updated *King Lear*.

A week later she wrote to say Provence was 'beautiful and lavish but too hot' and now she was home again in her house in Chelsea, and back with her play *Joyce's Women* and the problems the play presented were still unsolved.

In the evening she wrote again: 'So relieved to be back though I must isolate and have Covid tests, et cetera. Only you and I expire in the hot sun and people think we are "moaning". I have to get my strength back to finish this play. It's taking its toll.'

At the end of August, she wrote from Somerset; she was in a house she'd been loaned 'and have been here for five days working on Jas A Joyce (as he signed himself)'. Progress on her play was not as she wished. 'I so long to get it done but it's slow in gestation and I have 1000s of sheaves of paper all mixed up.' I'd heard this before. Fiendish stop-start forward motion producing panic and a plethora of notes.

This was also the way she worked, at least in later years. First, she accumulated and the text ballooned and then she sieved and the text reduced to its essence. It was a maddening process for her, and as the years advanced, working this way got harder: seeing those oceans of pages which she had generated rising around her, threatening to overwhelm and seemingly unamenable and intractable, induced terror (particularly with her eyesight and her vim declining). But she was always persevering; the pages were sifted and out of multiple versions and alternatives, the work emerged, as close to the ideal as she could get it. And because of the way it was made, her work acquired an authority. As a reader you were in no doubt everything was as it was presented because of a set of careful and complex decisions and there was no way anything could be presented except in the form in which it was finally offered. Every text was absolutely definitive, down to the last full stop. But the riddling work that preceded never showed; all traces of the effort in its making vanished and what was left gave no sense of the labour involved.

Her time in Somerset was almost over. She was returning to London the next day. The weather had been 'wonderful' and the gardens 'beautiful'; on one level she was sorry to leave; on another, though, she wasn't; she hadn't been able to work the 'advanced technology', which I knew meant she'd been unable to watch sport on TV. The Premier League had started on 13 August; once home she could lose herself in that. She signed off promising to ring once she got 'a bit clearer in the brain-pan (Synge's word for the head!)' Quoting the humorous sayings of writers whom she admired was something she did endlessly. It was also part of a lifelong programme – to undermine the lazy idea of writers as po-faced. Writers laughed too (or some at any rate did) and we had to remember that.

Mid-September: we spoke by phone; my wife and I were coming to London in mid-October. We would come and see her, I said. She liked this idea but feared a clash with her authorised biographer. He might be there in mid-October. Earlier in the year the appointment of this fabled figure had been mooted but I'd heard no more. Now he was about to visit and I was curious. What was the process? Authorised biographers, after all, didn't grow on trees.

'I wanted to appoint a biographer,' she explained. 'I decided it should be a man, not a woman, *and* an American, because that way I stood the best chance of being treated fairly. I wrote to Terrence Rafferty – he used to work for *The New Yorker* and he wrote about film – and I asked him who'd he recommend and he wrote back and said, "Could it be me, could I do it?" and I said "Yes."'

At the start of October she wrote one of her classic, breezy emails, short but full of suggestions. Her 'biographer had to postpone, as his poor wife got ill' so there was no clash as she'd feared and she could fit us in. She was 'looking forward' to seeing us 'and IF you can give me a bit of warning that would be great'. It seemed to me her diary anxieties were worsening. Increasingly, she needed to know down to the minute exactly when something would happen. She was sick and she was old and her body was no longer the biddable instrument it had once been. It would have its way and she couldn't stop it. But control of her calendar offered the comfort that there was still one area where she could have what she wanted.

Work continued: the update here was all reiteration; Joyce was 'in a heap up on the big table'. She hoped I was well. 'I have doctors this week and big drama with insurers,' she ended. The sign-off was another zinger. 'If only I could find an elixir for us all.' She meant the elixir of life, I presumed, which I thought an interesting thing to wish for seeing as she'd already found an elixir of sorts of her own (albeit it was temporary) – work. I write therefore I live, was her motto. By producing words, she could keep going, at least for a bit longer.

On Saturday, 16 October 2021, I went with my wife to see my mother at her Ovington Street home. We sat in the kitchen, she in the chair she favoured, the one she was in when she saw the fox. Her skin looked paper-thin as the skin of the old so often does. Her voice was low; I had to pay attention to catch her words. But her mind was sharp. She talked about *Joyce's Women*, which she hoped would be mounted in 2022, the centenary of the publication of *Ulysses*. She wanted John Tiffany, who directed the *Harry Potter* plays in the West End and on Broadway, to direct her play. She had written to him during Covid, she told us, and he had come to see her during the summer just past and he had given her some advice. He helped her to understand that she could put a film into the middle of the play, which had not previously occurred to her. She was hell-bent on getting this play put on and when she finished the play, she might write a novel, she said (she had an idea but didn't elaborate; all I gathered was that she had something in mind). As she talked about writing the novel she conceded she might not have the oomph required to write it when the time came. Again, I thought, the work is keeping her going, it's keeping her alive.

After about an hour, she led us out of her house. She walked with a stick; her steps were slow and careful but also anxiety-provoking; I was permanently anxious she might topple. We went up Walton Street to a Swedish café where, she said, she went every day for a decaffeinated coffee. We were going out to lunch, something I hadn't done with her for years.

We went in; the café's interior was plain: lots of wood, nice cutlery and plates, the smell of capers mingled with coffee. We ate smashed avocado and hummus, and she drank her decaffeinated coffee (she couldn't have the real stuff, it made her jiggy, she said), nibbled on a slim biscuit (she barely ate) and told us about a burglary at her house a couple of years earlier:

It was early evening, and she had an errand to run. She closed her front door – an ornate, heavily decorated and enormously heavy oak affair, which was now gone for reasons that later became clear – and the Yale clicked home. She inserted the key into the deadlock and then went to turn the key but the key wouldn't turn. She didn't understand why it wouldn't. It always did. She assumed something had caught or it needed oiling. It was a glitch; nothing to worry about. She would call Chubb later and they would come. The Yale had clicked shut, she thought, so it was safe to go on and leave the house for a bit and off she went.

When she got back, she found her beautiful front door lying on the floor of her front hall, exactly where she'd later seen the fox running past when she'd been sitting in the kitchen.

Lying? I checked. On the floor. Not just swinging open?

Yes, lying on the floor, she said, like a bridge into her own house.

She called the police. They came. They searched her house. Jewellery and other valuables were found to be missing. But her paintings hadn't been touched. If she'd returned later, however, the police were sure, she'd have found them gone. Oh yes, they'd have taken the paintings. These were professionals.

The police further assured her (what were they thinking? why say this to an old lady living on her own?) that the burglars had identified her house as worth breaking into and had had it under surveillance for days, even weeks. During this time, these experts made a note of her movements and habits and they only broke in when they knew she was out. (There was some comfort in this, I suppose; at least she wasn't at home when they broke in.) The police account of these housebreakers as pros prompted my mother to remember she hadn't been able to double-lock her front door when she went out just before the break-in. Might the mechanism have been tampered with, she wondered. The police checked the door. Yes, they said, the deadlocks had been disabled. With only the Yale in place it had been easier for the burglars to smash their way in. All part of the plan. They'd used rams applied simultaneously to the lock and the hinges, which knocked the door back and caused it to fall to the floor. Again, all part of the plan.

One of the policemen mentioned he'd always meant to read her but had never got around to it. She gave him a copy of something (and stupidly I forgot to ask what. That would have been a telling detail; what, of all the books she'd written, did she give the policeman as his starter text?). It was also characteristic, generous to a fault, always, regardless of the circumstances.

Lunch over, we returned to Ovington Street and saw her into her house. I examined the front door on the way in. Yes, this was not the door that was there when she moved into the house. This was a new high-security number and somehow, I hadn't noticed the change.

We said goodbye in the hallway. She seemed tearful and I felt she had something she wanted to say. Did she think she might never see us again? I didn't myself think it was the last time we would see each other. Her talk earlier about the play she was intent on finishing and then the novel she might write next were grounds for optimism. Perhaps she was just sad we were leaving. However, as she told us, just before we left, she was going to spend the rest of the day alone and writing and she was jolly pleased that that was what she was going to be doing. So, I was wrong on that account. And still, and still, there was something I couldn't fathom. And I never did.

One evening in the middle of November, I rang my mother. She was soldiering on with *Joyce's Women* (no change in terms of ambition) yet this was not the same person to whom I'd said goodbye after lunch in the Swedish café. Judging by the sound of her voice she was smaller. How I could know that from what I heard I don't know but I did.

I put the phone down. It was only a month since I'd seen her. How could this have happened? I was astounded. So much change in so short a span of time. Yet how could I be surprised? Didn't I know death sped everything up? Yes, I did, but knowing something in theory is quite different to meeting it in practice.

Early December. In the dream I am in a building (a church?) and there are whispering voices: I know it's my mother's funeral although the event bears no resemblance to a funeral. There's no coffin, for instance.

The moment I wake I hear my inner voice saying, 'Mother will die on Christmas Day . . .' This didn't feel clairvoyant; it was more of a factual, run-of-the-mill moment of prescience. A declaration of what was to come. I remembered our last call in November and my sense that she was getting smaller. Perhaps, I thought, though my unconscious understood I still didn't. I might apprehend her death, but I didn't comprehend it. Not yet. So, I needed to be reminded. Hence the dream.

Two days later an email pinged in. *Joyce's Women*, now finished, had been 'very well received by those who have read it but the director is the vital link' and the search was on for one. My understanding was that it was my mother's understanding that her play was destined for production. It struck me this was happening rather too fast (theatre was never so easy in my experience) but I didn't cavil. What did I know? Her play on the Abbey stage in Dublin: if it happened, that would be wonderful. This was a startling end to her 2021 and, I thought, a direct rebuke to the dream.

2022

At the end of 2021 the gods had finally started to smile on my mother and her play at least, and I hoped in 2022 they'd continue doing so. Rookie error. Never expect the gods to stay indulgent. They'll be squinting as soon as they can and so they were. By early January, when we spoke on a Sunday (we were back to speaking on the phone on Sundays) she was distraught about her play. Though its focus was Joyce's relationships with women, her play had been written to coincide with the centenary of the publication of *Ulysses* (1922) and must, she believed, be produced in the centenary year, 2022. Unfortunately, the Abbey didn't want to make a final decision till the summer and if they said no, then it was unlikely the play could go ahead in 2022. Theatre managements need long lead-in times and it wouldn't be possible to mount a production somewhere else in a few months. There was always 2023, of course, but the centenary would have passed by then so that would probably be it. The play wouldn't go on. *Joyce's Women* would join her other unproduced plays.

The play's marooning in no man's land, as she called it, took its toll. The following Sunday, when we were meant to talk, she wrote to cancel explaining she was 'hot and frenzied' and 'completely devoid of energy for the last few days, made worse by no sleep for 2/3 nights due to burning legs and feet which are a constant now'. She longed for relief but there was none, there being no news from the Abbey; I took this to mean that uncertainty and indecision about her play were having a direct physical effect. The body was expressing the anguish her mind was feeling. This was an ancient tradition.

The following Sunday she again wrote to cancel. Still no decision had been made by the Abbey. She was 'too weak to speak' and was 'going now to bed'. She concluded, echoing the clockwork conceit, 'I fear my life's engine is running out.'

The first Sunday in February there was a shift in mood. She wrote to say Tom Stoppard had read the play. He had liked it and not only had he liked it, he had also volunteered to introduce the play to other theatres with managements who might be interested if the Abbey wasn't. If *Joyce's Women* didn't have a life in Dublin, it might have a life elsewhere.

I had been reading *The Magic Mountain* (and told her how much I was enjoying it) and at her email's end she expressed delight in that fact, extolled Hans Castorp ('an idealist to the end'), praised Thomas Mann's artistry, and signed off, 'It's showing signs of spring.' I knew the explanation for this new tone, so different from the earlier emails; it was Stoppard's interest and his offer to act on the play's behalf. Yes, there was nothing to show, yet; no management had asked for rights but that didn't matter; an act of kindness had had a transformative effect.

On Monday 7 February, I was out on my morning walk. It was just before eight o'clock; it was cold and the sky in the east was brightening. The hilly fields I passed were quiet; only sheep (no cattle) and the sheep were mostly sitting very still. They looked posed. I was listening to *The Magic Mountain*, read marvellously by David Rintoul. I was on Chapter 5, the section called 'Research', where Hans Castorp on his balcony contemplates the winter scene outside the sanatorium:

> It had stopped snowing, the sky began to clear. The blue-grey cloud masses parted to admit glimpses of the sun, whose rays gave a bluish cast to the scene. Then it grew altogether fair; a bright hard frost and settled winter splendour reigned in the middle of November. The arch of the loggia framed a glorious panorama of snow-powdered forest, softly filled passes and ravines, white, sunlit valleys, and radiant blue heavens above all. In the evening, when the almost full moon

> appeared, the world lay in enchanted splendour, marvellous. Crystal and diamond it glittered far and wide, the forest stood up very black and white, the quarter of the heavens where the moon was not showed deeply dark, embroidered with stars. On the flashing surface of the snow, shadows, so strong, so sharp and clearly outlined that they seemed almost more real than the objects themselves, fell from houses, trees, and telegraph-poles. An hour or so after sunset there would be some fourteen degrees of frost. The world seemed spellbound in icy purity, its earthly blemishes veiled; it lay fixed in a deathlike, enchanted trance.[6]

Into my thoughts popped an idea. I had always known my mother would die but I had managed not to think about or accept the fact of her extinction by averting my gaze. I had done this because I didn't want to be frightened and worried and troubled and sad and a thousand other things. But as I had been walking, flooded with Thomas Mann's words, a shift inexplicably occurred and I'd stopped averting my gaze (or whatever it was I was doing to protect myself from the truth) and, just like that, I had seen the fact of her death, clearly and unmistakably. I was amazed, not by what had happened, but that I'd

---

6 *The Magic Mountain* by Thomas Mann. Trans. H. T. Lowe-Porter (London: Penguin, 1960), pp. 270–71.

managed to deny the fact until now. My talent when it came to denying death (at least my mother's) was legendary, spectacular. Or it was, it had been.

Three days later, Thursday 10 February, she wrote again. She was still excited by my reading *The Magic Mountain*; this was a characteristic enthusiasm; in a world of declining standards (which was the world in which she felt she lived) any engagement with literature had to be a good thing in her eyes; it was an act of resistance against philistinism and mediocrity. Thus, she wrote, 'hope you continue to love Mr Mann. Wait until you reach a section called "Snow" – mesmerising.' Her own news, delivered in the jaunty, throwaway, insouciant manner I'd come to know and admire, was tacked to the end: 'Off now to eye hospital. A lot of illnesses and nothing from Abbey. It must be Lent!' I found this cheery sign-off and the Lent gag elevating. A corner turned? Perhaps, I thought.

On Sunday 20 March there happened something which had never happened before: I got an email from her email address that was not written by her but by a friend. The day before she had tested positive for Covid, the friend explained; she was ill and she'd 'be in touch in the week'. And she was in touch. But not within the week. She was in touch that same day. 'In bed,' my mother wrote.

'Temperature down from yesterday. Have to stay in bed for at least four days. Energy nada.' So much for the corner turned.

Four days later I got her on the phone; she was breathless but alert; after a few minutes she had to abort the call and take herself back to bed. A few minutes later an email pinged in from her: 'I just got short of breath and faint, so am lying down,' she wrote, calculating this would put a stop on my worry.

Just over a week later the run of bad news was reversed. (The volatility of her life was bewildering.) On Thursday 31 March she reported that her play *Joyce's Women* now had a venue, the Abbey, and a director, Conall Morrison, and he had been to see her and casting was underway.

'Oh, lots of fun at Finnegans Wake,' she reported, in that familiar tone of exasperation mixed with exhilaration below which lay relief and pleasure in equal measure on account of the longed-for event, the production of the play, having commenced.

Our contacts over the spring and summer were brief. Her health was a preoccupation. On Saturday 23 July she reported, 'My real unverified fear is that the original cancer is back but that just might be ANXIETY.' She promised to let me know about this but didn't. A week later she was in the 'eye hospital . . . awaiting my turn which looks like it's going to be a while'. Her eyes would 'take eight weeks to get back to semi-normal,' she reported the following day, though what exactly the problem was she did not disclose. 'Life,' she conceded, 'is going to be very demanding and I hope to be able to do all that is being asked of me.'

In August she went to Dublin to attend rehearsals of *Joyce's Women*. She fell in the hotel where she was staying and fractured the bones of her right hand. She was right-handed, so, her ability to type and text were hindered. A new misfortune on top of the host of others. Ageing was not for the faint-hearted, as she often said.

I went to see the play at the Abbey at the end of September and after the show I sat with her in the upstairs bar. When I'd seen her earlier in the year (this was when she'd told me the story of the break-in at her house) she was a reduced version of the mother I knew, and now the mother beside whom I sat in the bar during the after-show scrum was a reduced version of that reduced version, plus her right arm was in a cast.

As we sat there, unable to communicate easily, because the noise was terrible and her voice was weak, I thought about Russian matryoshka dolls. Each time I met her, I realised, she would be a smaller version of what she had been the previous time, and this would continue until the point was reached when there was no smaller doll to come. Only I wouldn't know that, of course, at that moment. At what would turn out to be our last encounter I would believe there were more to come and only later, having failed to grasp that death was imminent, would I find I was wrong. This conceit was especially disorientating. I'm someone who needs order, who needs to know what is going to happen and when. I love teaching because I have a timetable and the timetable is locked and doesn't change. For some years now, I have known where I will be and what I will be doing, each year, each month, each week, each day, right down to the hour. Some may find this level of predictability intolerable but not me. I relish that I can anticipate and plan and stay in control. But death is inimical to calendrical and all other certainties. It will happen (there's no doubt about that) but when that will be you don't know till it happens, which, I was coming to see, troubled me nearly as much as the fact.

On Sunday, 1 October 2022 at 5 p.m. I rang my mother. She was disconsolate. *Joyce's Women*, she said, 'didn't get the reviews it deserved and the play will now not transfer'. Her broken hand would take ten weeks to mend. She couldn't type, write, or indeed do very much of anything. Because of the hand, because of her health, because of everything, she now had (and it was towards this revelation that she was building throughout the conversation) a 'carer'. She articulated this last word as if it was an obscenity but then of course it was, to her.

(The idea of her having someone in her house, in her space, doing things for her that she would ordinarily have done herself but now could no longer do, was a terrible concept and one from which she recoiled. She was always exceptionally private and an exceptional perfectionist; I knew any carer, no matter their tact and no matter their talent, would be found wanting and rebuffed.)

The carer card played, she continued listing her other difficulties. Her official biographer (Terrence Rafferty) came to interview her earlier in the day. He was late, she said. 'He was always late,' she added, though I knew that being as little as five minutes late was enough to disappoint her. She had made him coffee (difficult with her broken hand). He wouldn't drink it because it was cold (he'd thrown it away, she said) but it was cold because he was late. I was relieved I hadn't been present for this encounter. From this she moved to a general lament about manners. 'What has happened to everyone's manners?' she exclaimed. And then it was on to other things. She was short of money. She didn't have anything to write. She found everything difficult. After five minutes she ended the conversation. She couldn't go on. A few minutes later I got an email from her email address but written by a friend: 'I popped in to see Edna who is not well,' the friend wrote, 'and she is sorry that she was not able to have a happier conversation but hopefully another time.' Once again, she had had to clarify and signal that something better, hopefully, was to come. I found this need to get the uptick in as quickly as she always did rather marvellous.

Two weeks later, on Friday 14 October, she wrote to say her hand was in pain and she wouldn't know how well her bones had knitted (and if the pain was behind her) until 3 November when the plaster was to be removed. Her greater grief though was the play, *Joyce's Women*. It would not transfer to the West End as she had hoped. Its last night was the next night, Saturday 15 October. 'I am so sad it's closing but it was always only a three-week run. Waiting for rescue somewhere. Ring Godot!'

On the last day of October, I was asked to sound her out vis-à-vis her contributing to a forthcoming book about the Irish literary editor David Marcus, which The Stinging Fly Press was publishing. With someone's help ("This is being sent on my behalf as I cannot read the type') she wrote back before the end of the day.

She couldn't contribute, she began; 'it is out of the question. I am 92, almost blind, and trying against all the odds to write and earn my living . . . I am ill, very ill, and everything is a gargantuan effort. I barely remember David Marcus, wouldn't even know what to say.' None of this content nor the tone was unexpected. But the paragraph that followed did contain an enormous surprise. She had started a book about T. S. Eliot; this was not an expansion of her lecture, 'The Leap', but a brand-new text. It was going slowly and delivery would be three or so months later than she anticipated but she had something underway. Earlier in October she had complained she hadn't anything to write. Now, by the end of the month, she had and she had started. She signed off, 'As you can see, life is testing me hard', which was in harmony with the letter's despondent tone. But the other information in her reply contradicted this. Despite everything, she was back in harness, writing a book. Incredible.

2023

We flew to London in early January and on a cold Monday afternoon my wife and I tramped through the streets of Chelsea to my mother's house. The front door was on the snib, so we could enter without her having to get up to open it. She was waiting for us in the kitchen. She was on her chair, the one like a throne, and she stood up when we came in. The kitchen table in front of her was cluttered with books, papers, parcels, letters; clearly her temporary office. She complained – her feet, they were letting her down terribly. She could barely move but we would go up to the sitting room upstairs, she announced, and have drinks and nibbles. We began to prepare a tray at her direction (ice bucket, champagne, glasses, linen napkins, smoked salmon on buttered bread, Italian dry biscuits, blue cheese). She ordered the proper fish knives with flat blades and bone handles and the matching forks with the flat tines should be broken out of their velvet-lined canteen and put on the tray. We were having fish, so no other cutlery would do, she insisted.

Since childhood, I'd heard such orders being issued many times and memories of similar scenes flooded back. She'd inherited her domestic standards from her own mother and she wasn't about to let go of them now. Of course, I thought, propriety as a bulwark against the end. I decided it was a rather marvellous form of resistance.

My mother's Chelsea house was old and charming and idiosyncratic; the stairs to the first floor, where her sitting room was located, were steep and unfriendly and every tread had a different rise.

I climbed up, put down the tray and returned to the top of the stairs. Below me, as I looked down, I saw my mother and behind my mother my wife. My mother's ascent was slow, incremental. The woman who had walked us unsteadily to the Swedish café about a year earlier was gone and the replacement had even less capacity, even less mobility. The ascent was so difficult and slow and painful for her that the queenly kitchen scene of a few moments before – where she showed her determination to keep on keeping on despite the body's betrayal – acquired even more lustre.

Once she made the sitting room she sat on the long (and I always thought hideously uncomfortable) ottoman. Her back, I noticed, was ramrod straight. My wife took the prayer chair, which she'd bought in the auction room in Putney when we lived in Deodar Road. I sat on an old armchair with my back to the window facing the bookshelves. I always liked to sit here so I could look at the books. We nibbled. We sipped.

Outside the big casement windows behind, the light dimmed. A gloomy London dusk and a sense of something going, the tide flowing out. My mother asked my wife about her mother whom she'd never met. It was an unusual tack, I thought. If the scene had been photographed for a documentary and our desultory talk recorded, viewers would, I think, have decided that here were people gathered who weren't talking about what they knew they ought to be talking about. And we weren't.

When we left it was dark, the pavement slightly slippery. Wispy mist wraiths sliding about. A winter night. Walton Street: darkened small shops selling very expensive items; the melancholy peculiar to every upmarket retail area. Our mood low. We would have to return, we agreed. As soon as possible, we agreed. It was obvious we must. In two months' time. In early spring. Better weather. More light.

In Ireland I booked flights. Then I wrote to arrange the precise time we would come. Arrangements must always be made. She didn't like it any other way. In her email reply she proposed a Sunday. Early evening, 5.30 or 6 p.m.; the time when I often telephoned, I thought. We would have an hour or so and we would have 'a nice glass of champagne and some bits'. Her unchanging adherence to the highest standards of hospitality was reassuring, but there were new things in the email, which were anything but. She was 'a bit thrown by some domestic upset (money missing)' but couldn't elaborate, being 'too exhausted to go into it now. It's a saga.' This sent my mind spinning. Someone she knew had stolen from her? I knew better than to enquire though. There'd be no amplification.

'Bed now,' she ended, to prepare herself 'to battle tomorrow's chores and Eliot.' With her 'sight failing' and not being able to 'write at length' she had to get her sleep in so she didn't lose any time. In such circumstances, where she was having to conserve her energies, one might imagine she would have turned her face away from the world. But no, she hadn't. She'd been watching the news, closely. 'Poor Turkey and Syria and the Inferno all around. God help us,' she signed off.

Three days later this came from her:

'. . . in hospital. Had bad fall. Can't read or write.'

Knowing her aversion to the unscheduled phone call, I wrote suggesting I'd call at a specific time. Her response was unequivocal: 'No,' she wrote. She would contact me in 'a few days'.

Her communiqué, when it landed, began, 'I am afraid I will still be here for a spell longer,' which came across as an apology for the fact we wouldn't be able to visit her at her home as planned but would have to come to the hospital where she was recovering. It was in Battersea, and she was 'concerned about the journey' we'd have to make to get to her, there being no Tube to speak of, certainly not where her hospital was. She made all sorts of suggestions (maybe we take an Uber, or maybe our son Finn would drive us) and then apologised for not being 'more helpful' and for her hospital being south of the river (terra incognita for her). We could visit any time up to 7 p.m. but if it was 'too much hassle' crossing the Thames we could wait until she was back home, north of the river, in Chelsea.

Only in the second half of the email did she become personal. Things had 'been very rough' and she couldn't walk anymore though she dreamt she might one day in the future enjoy that freedom once again. She wanted us to know she didn't need 'flowers or gifts of any kind. Just a bit of cheer and news from beyond.'

She ended, 'As you can imagine, this lucid letter is being typed for me.'

When I entered my mother's room in the convalescent unit of the private hospital where she was recovering, I saw a silent, frozen figure with a white, shroud-like sheet stretched tight over the emaciated body. The stillness and the silence were the stillness and silence of the dead. I thought she was dead.

But that was also preposterous. If she were dead, wouldn't one of the many members of staff who were gliding up and down the corridor outside have stopped my wife and I on our way in, and told us?

My wife bent in, bent low, called my mother by her name, felt her temple, then cupped her palm and held it over her mouth.

'Yes,' my wife said. She could feel her breath, albeit faint, warm and present.

My mother revived, ate a morsel, sat up, grew animated (her spirits had risen entirely because of other human beings, us: it was instructive to see the effect of human contact) and she told us what happened before she sent the email telling us she'd had a fall.

Many weeks earlier she had been to hospital. Something to do with her eyes. Ninety-two-year-olds don't typically go to hospital appointments on their own but she did. She was determined to live independently as she always had. She had taken a taxi there. She got out and went into the lobby. She went to her consultant's office. She was seen. She returned to the lobby. This was the point at which 'it' happened. According to her account, the only way out of the hospital was through a rotating door, the kind you step inside and follow around and finally step out of on the other side. When you walk with a stick, and are unsteady on your feet, a revolving door is not what you want to negotiate. So, the question follows: was the rotating door really the only way out? Were there self-opening doors that weren't revolving? Was it possible that she hadn't seen the wheelchair-accessible sign pointing to the self-opening doors and so found herself taking the revolving door? I am normally quite adept at asking such questions but at the time we had this conversation I couldn't. Her approaching death had estranged me from my habitual interrogatory practice and stopped my intelligence from working. And there is one more thing to bear in mind about the lack of questions: it was only the end in which I had any interest at this moment, albeit I knew it already. I was so fixated on the climax, which was a catastrophe, that I ignored everything else.

She stepped unsteadily into the revolving door. One of the door's panels swept up behind her and threw her, like a cartoon character, into the street, where she landed, head first. No teeth were lost but the face, nose, skull and brain all took a pummelling.

As I listened and understood I started to seethe inwardly. How could a hospital have even one revolving entrance? Surely to God someone should have realised that it was a terrible idea to have a revolving door in a hospital where people, that's patients, who were surely not nearly as nimble as the architect who designed it had imagined, must meet disaster. And why was there nobody on hand to help patients like her through? The answer to that question, as I wearily reminded myself, was that institutions typically don't consider the needs of their users. Of course, there'd be the kind of door which would fell an old lady like a skittle at the front.

What else would a hospital have? I did ask if a complaint was raised but my query was batted away. Absolutely not, she said.

Her narration continued: after the fall, paramedics gathered around her; an ambulance came, she was admitted to A&E and from there she was brought to a dementia ward in the same hospital where she'd had her earlier appointment. After several very difficult days she transferred to this convalescent unit south of the river where she'd begun her slow and painful recuperation. Only it wouldn't return her to what she'd been, a person who lived alone and could take a taxi to a hospital because she had an appointment and could get into the hospital on her own, albeit with difficulty. When she returned to Ovington Street, she said, she would need not a drop-in carer, as previously, but an actual live-in carer because she couldn't move about any more like she had. She could no longer live independently. It was an admission I never thought I'd hear her make. Another marker.

We left, went north and crossed the Thames by the Albert Bridge. Death, in this case (or do I mean her case?) I was coming to understand, was less an event than a series of incremental reductions, with one capacity after another being taken away until at last, you came to the end – extinction. And like some wretched formula I needed for an examination but could not keep hold of in my mind, I had to keep relearning this, again and bloody again.

The entries I made in my journal over the following days were gloomy and morbid:

> The NHS has completely collapsed . . . All over London there is a general atmosphere of decay. . . empty shops, empty restaurants . . . The economy is in decline and all the government does is manage that decline . . . Everywhere I hear people complaining about everything not working, everything perishing, everything deteriorating . . . Housing, public transport, policing, everything has gone to the dogs . . . On my last morning, I overheard a father and daughter at breakfast; he can move to Portugal (Portuguese grand-parent I think and so has Portuguese passport). 'Dad,' she said, 'I can't go to Portugal but you can. Get out of England, Dad, it's a shithole, get out of England, move to Portugal and don't fucking come back.'

Was what I saw and recorded true or was it what I wanted to see because of what was happening? I know I felt hopping mad that my mother's deterioration had been accelerated by a visit to a place – a hospital – that was supposed to make things better not worse. Did I read across from the personal to the political? Did I extrapolate from my mother's ills to England's ills? I puzzled over this and I decided eventually that England's decline (which is a fact) and her dying had merged in my mind. Different sides, same coin. It was not only she who was dying.

Two days after St Patrick's Day I received an email from my mother; she was home and she had a live-in carer; 'a nutter' she added helpfully. No other details were forthcoming. We would speak in 'a few days'. I liked the sprightly, subversive tone and rejoiced that her sense of humour (acerbic, terrifying, lethal) appeared to be intact. One week later we had our usual Sunday evening telephone call. It was short and miserable. In my journal I wrote, 'Hopeless bleak truncated call with my mother; she is at the end of her tether.'

A few moments after we stopped talking, she sent me one of her characteristic emails of the kind she sent after talking: 'Sorry I couldn't chat . . . But I'm feeling awful. It will get better.'

On my last teaching day in April, it was not just the end of term but the end of the year, I left my office in the Oscar Wilde Centre for Irish Writing in Trinity College Dublin, slipped out the Lincoln Gate, crossed the road to Sweny's pharmacy and bought a bar of lemon soap, the same soap (allegedly) Leopold Bloom buys in *Ulysses* while waiting for a prescription to be made. I would shortly be on my way to London to see my mother and I would take it with me.

On Monday, 17 April, I showed up at 2 Ovington Street at 4.59 p.m. sharp. My appointment was for 5 p.m. I had one hour. The door was opened by the carer, Zoe. My mother was waiting for me in the sitting room upstairs. She looked fragile and startled; something about her of the fledgling sitting on the ground having fallen from its nest and looking bewilderedly about itself.

The last time I'd seen her she told me the grim story of her hospital fall and this afternoon, sitting in the sitting room in Ovington Street, she told me the whole story again, in her small voice, pale and shorn of its County Clare cadences: being pushed over by the revolving door and sent sprawling over the pavement; paramedics gathering around her; an ambulance coming; her being admitted to A&E, and then a dementia ward (in the hospital she'd been attempting to leave); and finally, after several very difficult days, transferring to the convalescent unit south of the river where she'd begun her slow and painful recuperation . . . and she told it *exactly* as she had told it before. She used the same words, the same phrases, the same constructions.

When she had started and I noticed she was repeating herself, I callously thought, *Is something wrong with her memory? Doesn't she remember she's already told me this?* But as she went on my mind went to Coleridge's 'The Rime of the Ancient Mariner' and the ghastly tale the Mariner is compelled to deliver to the Wedding Guest as he has been compelled to do many times before, describing his time at sea, his thoughtless killing of a blameless albatross, the carcass of which is hung around his neck by his fellow mariners, and the catastrophes the killing of the bird initiates; with the exception of the Mariner, the entire crew die. Some stories of hurt, I thought, the Mariner's no less than my mother's, are so deeply inscribed they can never be exorcised but only involuntarily repeated, though little good that does. Her experience of being flung to the pavement by the hospital's revolving door and her subsequent time in hospital was such an experience. Its details were gouged into her psyche; they might be retold but never jettisoned.

After she finished her account of her February fall, she moved swiftly to the present. 'No one warns you about old age,' she said. 'No one tells you that your body falls apart.' She said this in many different ways. And she was furious about the dereliction of those who had preceded her. How could they have failed her? I listened, perplexed. No one had spoken; she had received no warnings? Really. What about *Molloy*, *Malone Dies* and *The Unnamable* (the Beckett Trilogy), revered texts she'd obsessively read and re-read all her life – did these texts not hammer home the terrible truth that with ageing comes bodily disintegration? Seemingly not. Or at least, at this moment, the Beckett novels and everything else that had described the inevitable were discounted (it was as if they'd never existed), which left her free to rage against the world's failure to warn her. I thought of King Lear and decided I was coming to understand him better.

We moved finally to the present. Because of her body's incapacity, something must be done, and there were various plans afoot. One solution was the home in Highgate where Diana Athill (editor at André Deutsch and writer of many great books, my favourite *Instead of a Letter*) had spent her final years. It welcomed creatives. She might be comfortable in its artist-friendly embrace. My mother said she had visited Diana Athill there and it was okay. Then there was Raheen, the care home near Tuamgraney, the village where she was born and brought up; Raheen was where her aunt, my great aunt, Mama Delia and my aunt Eileen, her older sister, had gone at the end of their lives. I had visited both relatives in Raheen before they died there. As homes go, it was human and it was a lot cheaper than a care home in London would be. My mother wanted to know what I thought about Raheen. From experience I knew she alone would make the decision. Collective decision-making was never her forte. She always did it her way. So, in a situation like this the only thing to do was not take a position but to sound positive yet remain uncommitted. So, I gave an answer which I hoped sounded simultaneously positive yet didn't commit me either way.

But my non-committal answer didn't mean I didn't have any thoughts. I very much did. The Raheen plan was an indication of her foreknowledge; she knew she was going to die and she preferred to die on Irish soil, a few miles from where she was born. Though I could see the logic I thought it was too late now to move back to Ireland, although I took care not to be emphatic about this. She hadn't the strength to travel and besides the wrench from the familiar (from her house and her books, her things and the people she knew and most importantly of all, from London) would finish her. At this stage it was better she stayed where she was.

Zoe the carer came and my mother said to Zoe she could go for the night (an order couched as an offer). Zoe said she was quite happy to stay and, it was my understanding, she had also been paid for her overnight duties, but my mother was adamant. No, no, she should go, home to her own kith and kin. Zoe left. I heard the front door slam and now I felt I could ask. Why did she want Zoe to go? The answer she gave was that Zoe was 'too heavy'. She wanted light. Then the bell went, three sparkling rings (clearly an agreed code) and then I heard a voice shouting up from downstairs, 'Hello, Edna, it's me, it's Nina!' and a moment after Nina was there in the doorway, small, sweet, smiling. I knew Nina. I had met her before. Nina was a hairdresser my mother liked very much and, I now discovered, she hired her informally on an ad-hoc basis, to provide care, which was what she'd be doing for my mother this evening. That was why she sent Zoe away. She'd booked Nina. She didn't want heavy Zoe; she wanted light Nina. Her prerogative, of course.

Nina's arrival meant I must leave. And I'd had my hour anyway – my mother hour, which was just like the therapeutic hour as I was coming to think of it, for it was just as rigidly enforced.

I left and walked away. I chose a circuitous route to where I was going through Chelsea's back streets. Small, crooked old houses, nice gardens with clean gravel and sandstone paths. Beethoven's 'Fleur de Lis' being practised on a piano in a house. London lime trees with little green leaves, iridescent and magical, starting to show. Low sun slanting on brickwork, all buttery and warming, its heat on my face even as my head churned with tumbling thoughts and terrors.

My phone pinged; I knew who it would be and got the phone out; my mother getting the last word in.

'Thank you so much for coming all this way. It truly lifted my heart. Also, the gift of Bloom's soap . . . My love to the flock.'

I was on my way to meet my children. Hurrah, hurrah, I thought.

I was no sooner back in Ireland than I was on to my mother to arrange another visit. A desolate reply by return almost immediately: 'Am sick all night will reply later.' This was followed soon after by a second, longer, even more hopeless message: 'Very bad night and in bed now. It's all getting harder . . .'

By day I was marking scripts, the scripts of students I taught at Trinity. By night I was sleeping badly. One night I dreamt my mother was going to die on my birthday which was coming up in August. I told my wife in the morning. This was no premonition; she was sure of that, she said. This was me imposing a pattern onto chaos, she said. As human beings are wont to do, she added, with customary tact. Yes. I was one of those human beings, as well we knew, who has spent his life imposing patterns in order to subdue the unruly inexactitude of lived experience and so, because another's death is so intolerable precisely because it's so disordering and unpredictable, of course I'd come up with a death date. It gave me a cut-off point, something to hold on to. And it was a good one too. Numinous. Just what one would expect of the unconscious.

The last Sunday of April. I drove my wife to Knock airport so she could catch a flight to Heathrow. She was going to London to see my mother. I was not. I was staying at home. I had work.

The flight left at one. My wife would see my mother that evening at 6 p.m., the time I usually telephoned. Because my wife would be with my mother I did not arrange to ring as I usually did. My mother, I knew, wouldn't want to be bothered while she entertained her guest. And besides, my wife would be ringing later and I would find out everything I needed to know then.

My wife did ring. Your mother's voice is different, my wife said. She is definitely different, too. She is less than before. Death is quite close, my wife said. She also said my mother had expressed relief that I hadn't phoned. 'She's too tired to take calls,' my wife said. 'Everything is too much.'

This was no sooner finished than my mother rang. 'The battery is running down,' she said, and rang off.

Had our hour on 17 April been our last meeting? I spent the rest of the evening unable to settle. The feelings of disquiet were hot, scorching, aggravating, needling and they just kept prodding.

I had long mother dreams all night. I didn't remember them when I woke on May Day. Only that I had had them. The feelings of the previous night were still there only they were not quite as strong; they were hot embers in the hearth the morning after rather than the raging fire of the night before.

The next day, Tuesday 2 May, my wife rang. She had seen my mother again. The night before; she'd visited for two-and-a-half hours (a record). My wife boiled their conversation down to a single pithy sentence. 'She's terrified of dying alone,' my wife said.

As soon as I finished talking to my wife, I booked flights to London for the end of May. And that night I had the following dream:

I must go somewhere to teach . . . somewhere like the Arvon Foundation. It's in the English countryside. I'm sure I can remember the way. I set off by car. I grow increasingly confused on the motorway (which is uncannily like the M4). I pull off and go to a town. I find an arts centre. They will help, I think. But I've now forgotten where I'm going, its name, its location. The amnesia is terrifying. The art centre's employees know I write, know I am a writer. Several approach, bearing their unpublished and unpublishable manuscripts. Can I help them find an agent or a publisher? I ring my wife. Tears. Grief. Panic. 'I am lost,' I say. 'Utterly lost.'

I know I saw my mother at the end of May, for an hour, but what happened then, what was said, what I felt, I have no idea. I didn't write the meeting up in my journal. In fact, I wasn't writing anything up in my journal; all the way through May and all the way through June, I didn't go near my journal at all. Didn't want to? Couldn't? I don't know. It's gone.

On Sunday 9 July I spoke to my mother at six. There were two themes:

One, she can't go on but she must go on. What she actually said was, 'I can't go on. I'll go on.' Straight out of Beckett's *The Unnamable.*

Two, she detests T. S. Eliot about whom she's writing a book.

This conversation rolled on as she expanded on her two themes. Then, I heard voices. 'Ah,' she said. It was my brother and his son who had let themselves into my mother's house while she was speaking to me on the phone.

'Oh hello,' I heard her saying to my nephew, her grandson, on whom I knew she doted. 'Is it a kissing day?'

I heard my nephew demurring and my mother pressing and joshing. It was an extraordinary turnaround; in a nanosecond she'd switched from the gloom of Beckett to the sparkle of Richmal Crompton's *Just William* series, with her playing the part of one of the matrons who suborn William Brown throughout the stories and my nephew taking the role of Crompton's young hero.

I put the phone down. I remembered her reviving in the convalescent home when my wife and I appeared. Human beings can have that effect, I reminded myself. Contact can be transformative. And then I remembered all the times when, in various prisons, I had visited men who were in solitary and the weird, sunken, withdrawn way they had of presenting after the door was unlocked and I stepped into the cell, and how, as we talked, they would rise slowly and return (albeit only partly) to their original human truth. Hadn't I seen something similar with my own mother? My mother's current life, I thought, was not the exact equivalent of what a man in solitary undergoes but it was not so different either. Her current lived experience was a civil, non-penal version of solitary. And she was not the only one suffering this way. The old everywhere (certainly in the affluent, western world) were becoming diminished versions of themselves in their non-penal version of solitary that we've invented for them. This was one of the weird new truths of this weird new world I'd fallen into.

I spent the following week working on my book, *A Cold Eye* ('I feel the MS is inching towards completion,' I wrote in my journal) but my mother's dying was always there, on the edge of my thoughts, a stone in the shoe pressing on the tender sole.

A couple of days before we were due to go to London to see my mother I rang. She answered the phone and her words tumbled out pell-mell . . . She was on morphine. Everything was going wrong. Her body was letting her down. She was in hospital because of another fall. (I hadn't known.) But that wasn't the problem. It was something new. (She wouldn't say what.) She had medical insurance but now she needed to be in hospital they (the medical insurance people) cavilled and quibbled, the bastards. Six hours on the phone she'd spent and only for a kind nurse who'd admitted her without the insurer's approval she'd still be out in the street. There was a nice doctor in the hospital and when she told him something (again the mystery, the withholding) he was startled. Oh, I didn't know about that he said. That was doctors for you. They only knew what they knew. They couldn't see beyond their specialism. So far, nothing unexpected. Insurers were woeful and medics not much better. Then this. The nice doctor who didn't know much turned out to be an ally and, despite the long litany of troubles and hospital stays, he had given permission: Monday she could sleep at home in her house in Ovington Street and on Tuesday she could go to Cornwall in a car with a driver. She knew I was in London on Tuesday and Wednesday and would like to see her but, she continued, she didn't have the strength to dovetail my visiting with her travelling to Cornwall. She was exhausted, she explained, so much so it precluded my visiting. She was galloping now. Six months ago, she had hoped to live so she could write two things (*The Hermit Thrush* – this was the title she'd lighted on for her book on T.S. Eliot – and a novel based on the Medea; this last was a completely new piece of information; I'd never heard anything about this putative novel before) but now she felt so battered – and depressed (this was the first time she'd ever used that word in my hearing) – she had no wish to go on with life or with literature. *The Hermit Thrush* contained flashes of brightness but a good deal of sludge, she said, and she couldn't let it be published unless it was perfect and seeing as now she wouldn't get to be able to make it perfect it probably wouldn't be published. She would never start the Medea novel. She would die first. Our meeting would have to wait till the autumn. She was grateful I'd called. She had tried to order a glass of wine with her evening meal (an omelette) but the nurse had informed her no alcohol was allowed in the hospital. A hospital where she was paying a fortune. And they didn't let you have a glass of wine. It was the end of the world. She wished me well. Goodbye . . .

I put the phone down and remembered Susan Sontag's account in *Illness as Metaphor* of her journey from the kingdom of the well to the kingdom of the ill or sick and as her son puts it in *Swimming in a Sea of Death*, 'her acquisition . . . of that second citizenship'.[7] My mother had heretofore womanfully striven to keep to the kingdom of the well and whenever the official with her new passport detailing her new citizenship (just issued) in the kingdom of the ill or the sick had bearded her, she'd always declined. She wasn't having the new passport, no matter

7 David Rieff, *Swimming in a Sea of Death: A Son's Memoir* (London: Granta, 2015).

the evidence to the contrary. But following the latest admission to hospital there'd been an alteration in her position, or so I surmised. She'd taken the new passport. She'd left the well and joined the ill, the sick. That's why she used the dreaded word 'depression' in my hearing for the first time ever, although I recognise she may have used it with others at an earlier point.

About an hour after the call ended, I received an email from my mother. She was sorry she had been 'so down'. 'Pain and worries have just beaten me up,' she explained, 'BUT I pray to get a bit better and more disposed towards people and situations. I am sorry not to see you but there will be another time . . .'

Perhaps in the intervening hour, I thought, she'd summoned the passport-issuing official back and returned her new passport to him saying, *Here, I don't want it. Keep it!*

'Very weak but maybe will recover,' she wrote to me in mid-July as she was about to set off for Cornwall in a hire car with a chauffeur. She was having a holiday and staying in a rented house.

Once she was ensconced, glad messages began to flow across the Irish Sea about the beauty of the house and the warmth of the Cornish sun and the balm of the Cornish air, which she praised fulsomely and repeatedly as 'clean'. Despite her sensitivity to the cold, she was a fully paid-up 'fresh-air fanatic' all her life and a true believer that air, providing it was fresh and preferably turbulent (stormy sea air always a favourite) had unique medicinal and restorative powers. The right kind of air, here what she called 'clean' air, could achieve wonders that she believed ordinary common-or-garden air couldn't. Her heightened and complex responsiveness to the natural world was always part of her way of being in the world and it was still intact.

At the end of the month she returned to London. 'A bit low in energy,' she wrote to me, and she promised to contact me in a week. I wasn't prepared to wait a week. I emailed, proposing I ring. 'Let's wait. I'm sick again,' she replied. Start, stop, down and down and down it goes, I thought.

August was a blizzard of temporary hospital admissions and fraught returns to Ovington Street: carers came and went; I was an onlooker, watching from Ireland. This was the only entry I made in my journal during that period, but it seems in hindsight representative:

> I rang the hospital to see about my mother at eight. I got put through to the ward where I gathered that the mailbox was full and I couldn't leave a message. I was told to ring back at nine when there would be someone to answer the phone.

> I did ring at nine, on the dot, and I got a nurse. My mother was sleeping, the nurse said. She was going home later. Then she qualified. My mother would be going home later if she would agree to a care package; unfortunately, as the nurse put it, she wasn't engaging.

I know I went to a yoga class after I had made this phone call and I know throughout the class I was fitful and unfocused. I wanted to know what was going to happen in the next few hours and I wanted to know (even as I knew this was a question to which there was no answer) how long she had to live. At the end of the class, during the relaxation part, it occurred to me, stretched on the mat, breathing in, breathing out, that waiting for the unpostponable I was never in the moment or the present anymore. Never. I was always elsewhere as I waited for what was looming. Heightened expectation was the thief and a spoiler of everything, and it had quite worn me out. I wondered then if Louis MacNeice in *Autumn Journal* described something similar as the unpostponable world war loomed in the late 1930s. I couldn't remember. And perhaps I was being fanciful. A personal calamity is very different to a political one.

Towards the end of the month I emailed: 'Thinking of you of course. And wondering how you are?'

Her reply by return: 'Slowly it goes. Some days can't move. Waiting for miracle. Excuse brevity.'

I immediately booked flights to London at the start of September for myself and my wife.

The first Friday in September about 4 p.m., my wife and I set off on foot from Old Church Street in Chelsea, where we were staying, for my mother's house. We had no definite appointment but we had a plan. In St Luke's Gardens, boys on scooters brushed past, pursued by nannies pushing prams. On the grass a circle of children on blankets and a birthday cake and a blackboard and some sort of game supervised by another nanny. Moments from an Elizabeth Bowen story. London plane trees and scrubby London grass, surprisingly green given it was so dry. A woman with a pink iPhone on a bench in tears. More children and more nannies. The children white, the nannies not.

A small boy with a stick ran by.

'Put that down,' his nanny ordered.

'Why?'

'Put it down.'

The boy sped away brandishing his stick like a sword.

'She's forgotten,' said my wife. 'Every boy needs his stick.'

We got to Ovington Street and found it cordoned off with tape and barriers. PAs with clipboards and stopwatches. A chuck wagon parked at the kerb outside my mother's house, beside which large men stood drinking tea and not talking. An actor on a stool being made up, the make-up woman's brush strokes tender and careful. A camera on rails, being moved up and down as a complex shot was rehearsed. A film crew at work, getting ready to shoot something.

My wife went off to buy my mother a gift. I waited outside my mother's house. All the blinds were drawn and the house was silent. I thought of 'The Sisters', the opening story of Joyce's *Dubliners*, and the narrator's description of regularly passing a shut-up Dublin house where a death is ongoing and the extraordinary conclusion of the opening paragraph: 'Every night as I gazed up at the window I said softly to myself the word paralysis. It had always sounded strangely to my ears, like the word gnomon in the Euclid and the word simony in the Catechism. But now it sounded to me like the name of some maleficent and sinful being. It filled me with fear, and yet I longed to be nearer to it and to look upon its deadly work.'

On the other side of the street, across from where I stood, the actor (now made up) clipping along the pavement, the camera on a dolly ahead of him and looking back. Nothing about what I was seeing told me what type of film this was . . . romance, comedy, thriller . . . I half-thought about engaging someone with a clipboard and a stopwatch and asking, 'What is the film?' I've always had a certain ability when it comes to striking up conversations with strangers. But I hadn't the energy this afternoon, I realised. Or the inclination. I just wanted to get in and see my mother who I knew was inside her silent, shut-up house.

Around the corner shot the diminutive figure of Nina, as expected. She had the house keys, as expected. She'd let me in. Nina smiled and produced the keys on a chain. We went down the side passage. She unlocked the front door and we went in. The house was warm, too warm. 'Miss Edna,' Nina called up the stairs. 'This is Nina and your son.' 'Your mother is in bed upstairs,' she told me. She would just run up and check on her. Nina shot up the twisting stairs and across the landing. I heard her footsteps in the bedroom and her voice, light, pliant, calm and silvery. Then she came back out to the landing and told me to come up.

I climbed the rickety stairs and went through the door into a room I had never previously entered, ever, not once, in all the years my mother had lived in Ovington Street. Her bedroom was dark. Overheated. There were shelves crowded with religious icons – so many I was reminded of Greek Orthodox churches I have visited – and hanging on the wall a pen-and-ink of a melancholy female nude, sitting in a chair supporting her head on her hand. I remembered when my mother returned from Holland with this drawing which she had bought and feeling the sadness that pulsed from it then and which was still pulsing from it now.

My mother was sitting up in bed in a polka-dot cotton nightgown. Tousled hair. Baffled manner.

'It's awful,' she said in a papery voice. 'No one warned me.'

There was no reply to this; I sat down to wait. I stayed very still.

'I went to see a doctor,' she continued. 'He brought me into his empty consulting room. He said, "I'm going to tell you the truth now. You have no right to come here." That's what he said and I said, "You should not be talking to me like this. Why do you not show me any pity? I am in desperate need of help and this is what you say?" He was a bastard. He was the cruellest bastard I've ever met and I've met some bastards, I can tell you.'

I could hear Nina and my wife talking quietly on the landing outside.

'I have a carer,' my mother said. 'She comes here and she says, I want to help you. She wants to help me. But what can she do for me? She can do nothing. Nothing, nothing, nothing.'

'One after the next, Miss Edna dismisses them,' I heard Nina saying outside. She meant the carers. She'd been following my mother.

My wife came in. My mother repeated the doctor story to her word for word, concluding, '. . . He was the cruellest bastard I've ever met and I've met some bastards, I can tell you.'

But then she went on:

'And do you know what he said then? He said, "Stop working." "You're ridiculous," I said. "I have to work. It's all I can do."'

I thought she'd stop there, but she didn't. She went straight on. 'I need a glass of wine,' she said to me. 'But it must be in a small glass. A glass of cold white in a small wine glass. There's a bottle of Sauvignon Blanc open in the fridge in the kitchen. Fetch me the wine in a small glass and a big glass of wine for yourself, will you?'

I did as she asked, returned, handed her small glass to her. She took a sip, smiled.

'Superb.'

In the kitchen downstairs Nina and my wife nattered away cheerfully as they prepared my mother's evening meal.

'Would you do something for me?' she whispered.

'Of course.'

She pointed at the tube of ointment on the table. Would I apply some to her temples, she asked. It was for the shingles, she said. Still torturing her.

I put the unguent on. Her skin was hot. The ointment smelt of lavender. When I finished my finger-ends were shiny and warm. I went back to my wine. It was now warm too.

My mother took another sip from her small glass. 'I'm finished,' I heard her say. 'I've had enough. I cannot go on.'

She stared at the corner of the ceiling on the other side of the room.

'Emily Dickinson says there is an emerald coast. Did you know that?'

'No.'

'And I can see the emerald coast. The emerald coast is just there . . . Beckoning me to step forward . . . to step ashore . . .'

Nina appeared and told my mother she was making her a crêpe with spinach. It was in the oven, cooking. My mother took Nina's hand, kissed it, pressed it to her heart.

'I love you, Nina,' she said. 'How can I be without you, Nina? I couldn't manage without you, Nina. No one understands me but you, Nina.'

Nina regarded her sceptically, even warily. Something was passing over my mother's face, which she saw and now I saw. A storm was coming.

'When Nina brings the food,' she started fiercely, 'you will go, Carlo. I have to write a very diplomatic letter to a doctor and I can't write and Nina will have to type it for me and I can't have anyone here when that's happening.'

'Of course,' I said.

But she wasn't finished. She was just beginning.

'I hate emails, I fucking hate emails. I want them out of my fucking life. I want them abolished. I never want to see another fucking email for as long as I live, which won't be long. God grant me this wish – no more fucking emails for the time remaining. Now, go and call your wife to come and say goodbye.'

I picked up my glass. I would take it down to the kitchen, rinse it and put it away.

'I hope that's not my glass,' she said quickly. 'I hope you're not taking my wine away.'

Later, my wife and I found ourselves on Queen's Gate, a wide street of huge, stucco-clad houses. As we ambled, we glanced sideways, now at luxurious interiors with glass tables and stainless-steel lamps, now at badly lit, high-ceilinged rooms filled with bunk beds, flimsy laundry racks heaped with drying clothes, rickety tables supporting Belling stoves on which pots steamed, tended by exhausted-looking African or Asian women. These, we guessed, were some of London's domestic servants at the end of their day's work in their cramped, over-crowded dormitories. These women were not flourishing and their exploitation was palpable.

In *Memoirs of a Fox-Hunting Man* (the first volume of Siegfried Sassoon's *The Complete Memoirs of George Sherston*), Sassoon's alter-ego, George Sherston, having just boarded a train at a London station, notes as he steams away: 'I was glad to avert my gaze from the dingy and dilapidated tenements and warehouses which we were passing. Poverty was a thing I hated to look in the face.'[8] It takes service on the

8 Siegried Sassoon, *The Complete Memoirs of George Sherston: Memoirs of a Fox-Hunting Man* (Faber & Faber, 1937), reissued 1972, p. 73.

Western Front and the experience of the ordinary infantry man's suffering to lift Sherston into consciousness and to teach him 'that life, for the majority of the population, is an unlovely struggle against unfair odds, culminating in a cheap funeral'.[9] The domestic workers in their Queen's Gate rooms were, I thought, part of a current immiserated majority whose lives of struggle end as Sassoon describes.

On their first publication, Sherston's confessions about his youthful recoil from the less well-off were discomforting even if widely practised. You really should not hate to see the poor, not if you wanted to be considered as a fully rounded human being. But in the twenty-first century, when money is back, I wondered if it was still the case that we would think this kind of knee-jerk disdain is unacceptable. Or are the values of Sherston, when he was in his pleasure-seeking unenlightened phase, in the ascendant again? Would it matter now if someone said, 'I hate to see the new servant class in their dormitories in Queen's Gate when I'm strolling home at night'? It was my sense that this sort of pose is more common, more acceptable. It was also my sense that my mother witnessed and abhorred the adoption of this pose. Sufferers should always be seen, she thought.

---

9 *The Complete Memoirs of George Sherston: Memoirs of an Infantry Officer*, ibid., p. 425.

Before I went to sleep I found the Emily Dickinson poem, 'A Route of Evanescence' (1489), that my mother had referred to earlier:

> A Route of Evanescence,
> With a revolving Wheel –
> A Resonance of Emerald
> A Rush of Cochineal –
> And every Blossom on the Bush
> Adjusts its tumbled Head –
> The Mail from Tunis – probably,
> An easy Morning's Ride –

When I read the compact eight lines, I fathomed individual words ('cochineal', 'emerald', 'blossom') but not others. What was the Mail for Tunis? I knew the word 'evanescence' refers to passing out of existence, and that death is in the mix; but how exactly? I could make no sense of the piece as a whole. And how my mother could have got from this poem with its elliptical words to the conceit of the emerald coast where the souls of the dead went, I had no idea. But I loved the notion of an emerald coast – (somewhere in the Caribbean perhaps? coconut trees, warm sands, a lovely sea) – which was much nicer than the melancholy banks of the Styx where Charon waits with his boat to row you across as long as you can pay, and I was consoled that it was not only my mother who might end up here but all the other people I knew then who were approaching their end (and who would die in 2024 along with her, making the year's tally of death, for me, four).

And weirdly, the next day, which was Saturday, when I was alone, for my wife had gone off to see her own family, there they all were, everyone I had imagined ending up on the emerald coast. First there was an email from G, a poet and colleague at Trinity in Dublin. Then I went up to a nursing home in St John's Wood to see K, who had been my tutor at the National Film and Television School in the 1970s. Later, I went to East London to see another G, an artist who I'd worked with in film and who had designed many of my book jackets. While I was talking to G about his illness my phone rang. It was my mother.

'I have made a terrible mistake,' she said in the special tone that she reserved for calamities. Her carer that morning was a gardener, she explained. She didn't like her so she'd told the woman she could go away and garden and the woman had fled, delighted to be released, leaving my mother delighted in her turn that she'd sent the woman off to do what she loved to do, which was to care for her plants. But no good deed goes unpunished. My mother fell on the stairs and now the carer had been dismissed there was no one to help her to get up. An hour-and-a-half, according to my mother's account, it took her to inch from the stairs to the front door, which now was open because she'd managed to open it, and from there she had got herself to the kitchen and her phone. And now what she wanted to know was this: would I come to her?

I found her sitting on her throne chair in the kitchen. She was freezing. She sent me to find her coat. I found it and returned and spread it over her shoulders. 'I have made a terrible mistake,' she said. She then again told what she had already told me on the phone about sending the carer away to her gardening duties and then falling.

'Was there cheese in a jar in the fridge?' she asked. I went to look but couldn't see any.

'Help me up,' she said. 'Get me to the fridge.'

I got her to the fridge and she found the cheese in the jar that she wanted.

'There!' she shouted triumphantly. 'Look harder next time.'

She asked me to fetch her charger from her bedroom because her phone battery was dead. I fetched the charger and put her phone on charge and it pinged. She texted her evening carer, Miranda, asking her to come early and the carer texted back.

'I need to go to bed,' she said. 'Then you will go.'

'I will stay till the carer arrives.'

'No. You will leave.'

We crept out to the stairs, she inching up with me pushing from behind. Every time I pushed, she lifted a foot slowly and placed it on the tread above. Step by step we went. Incremental, painstaking work. Her body was pitifully slight. If Willie, I thought, Winnie's old husband in Beckett's *Happy Days,* had ever managed to stand up in the play whilst his wife talked brightly from inside the mound, this is exactly how he'd have moved.

We reached the landing. She went ahead into the bedroom. Gradually she lowered herself onto her bed. She stretched out. She looked stranded and ungainly. Not at rest. She complained she was cold though the room was as hot as General Sternwood's orchid house with its 'meaty' flowers and 'boiling alcohol' odour at the start of Raymond Chandler's *The Big Sleep*. I folded blankets over her. She went utterly still. She looked relieved. She said she'd be okay. She told me to go. I went downstairs. In the kitchen I thought of leaving a note for Miranda, asking her to stay for the hours she was contracted to work and not to leave, whatever my mother said, but I decided against doing so.

The next day, Sunday, we went back in my mother's house, my wife (now back from visiting her family) and I. We found her in the sitting room.

'I've taken two hours to get ready,' she said.

She wore a clean nightdress and her face was made up.

'The Pope buried Yevgeny Prigozhin,' she said.

This was news to me. I had no idea the Russian leader of the Wagner mercenary group, recently killed when the aeroplane in which he was flying was blown up, was a Catholic. I typed 'Prigozhin buried by Pope' into Google search on my iPhone but nothing came up. What did emerge was Prigozhin had recently been buried at a private cemetery on the outskirts of his home town, St Petersburg. Ah, I thought, listening to the news she heard *St Petersburg* as *St Peter's* (an easy mistake) from which she jumped to the assumption that the Pope officiated, which she figured was an anti-Putin gesture. I offered my theory, assuming she'd be pleased the tangle had been untangled. I was wrong. She, who was always so accurate when it came to current affairs, now understood she had got her facts wrong. This infuriated but it also desolated her for she saw her error as further proof of the decline that deepened and darkened day by day as her powers left her, and which would culminate, as described by Philip Larkin in his great searing poem about death, 'Aubade', in nothingness and extinction; in the poet's reckoning, not existing after existing is the worst of the worst. Watching her face as she processed what had happened, I saw the double terror, the terror of being extinguished and the terror of knowing the future was never-ending extinction, for ever. When we left, she was weeping quietly.

*

A couple of days later she sent the usual rectification email as she always did after a low. 'Sorry was in such a low state last Sunday. I had a temp of 102 and felt woeful. Apologies to you.'

Time after time into the abyss she fell, and time after time she pulled herself out again.

The Sunday following, I sent my traditional supplication:

'Good afternoon. Shall I phone later?'

The response:

'Edna is very weak today she will call in a day or two.'

I responded in the usual way; I booked tickets to London at the end of October.

Over the following days and weeks occasional messages pinged in; some were short, extraordinarily compressed telegraphic messages, which put me in mind of the graffiti daubed on walls I have sometimes seen in Belfast and elsewhere, non-political, non-partisan, non-doctrinaire but entirely personal revelations of sufferings which the writer had to express, while others were slightly longer statements consciously written in the knowledge that time was finite and some things had to be said before time ran out:

'I am only able to sleep. Forgive.'

'Still in hospital and very frail . . .'

'I hope you are okay. A bit too weak to chat.'

'The day started okay but an emergency struck.'

'Sorry for all the confusion but it has not been a calm time . . . I somehow had an LSD session [by which she meant a flashback; this was not uncommon following her single experience of taking the drug] which has thrown me considerably . . . I am peculiar to say the least . . . I am on twenty pills a day and do not know where I am . . . you are welcome for a fairly quiet visit.'

'Forgive my neglect but I am simply not able to see or to type. Things are not improving.'

'Yes, I'm sick my love and not sure what the future is bringing to me. I got help sending this as I cannot see anymore but wanted you to know I love you.'

The doctor seen during the period she sent these messages informed her further treatment would be fatal (though what exactly that treatment was I did not know; such facts she kept to herself, or, at any rate, she did not share with me) and moreover that she could not return to Ovington Street and live independently. It was hard to know which was the worst part of this news.

On the last Saturday in October my wife and I entered a delicatessen on the King's Road in Chelsea. It was one of those exclusive establishments with only a handful of beautifully packaged, very expensive items for sale – biscotti, dark wholemeal pasta, organic wine – artfully arranged at wide intervals on the shelves.

My wife asked for a portion of cheese but was told it couldn't be sold to her.

'My mother-in-law is in a convalescent hospital,' said my wife, 'and we're going to see her now and she craves savoury, salty things. I thought if I could bring a sliver, it might give her a lift.'

The victualler, tall, middle-aged, his skull a fuzz of grey, launched into his story. His own mother, 86, put in a home by his brother, no discussion; she too craved the savoury, the salty. He could relate to that. He would ignore the rule and sell us the cheese, though why he couldn't sell us the cheese in the first place remained undisclosed.

We walked off with our cheese and one or two other things in lovely little bags. It was autumn and the Chelsea pavements were slippery with wet leaves, which looked like pieces of torn cardboard. On the Albert Bridge as we trod south, we looked down at the Thames and saw the water was not black but green. On the corridor of the convalescent home (it was the one we'd previously visited) humming machines, whispering nurses, a succession of doors opening onto rooms inside which we saw one old convalescing person after another. A nurse, Fatima – Somalian, I later discovered – told us my mother was sleeping but had left instructions she was to be woken when we arrived. Fatima went into my mother's room and woke her and came out and told us we could go in. We entered. My mother lay on the bed, incredibly slight and incredibly straight, with her arms outside the covers. I had never seen a person so straight, so rigid. I thought of a doll in its box. Unlike when we last were here, there was a faint sound of breathing. Her mouth was open, her eyes were open. She began to whisper. We bent down. She spoke in fits and starts but she was coherent; it was clear she knew what she wanted to get across and she would not be stopping until she had. It was about her conditions. She had to tell us. This hospital was terrible. The staff were cruel, and monstrous, intemperate and rude and churlish. They did not know how to care.

Fatima appeared and my mother swerved away from invective and into cordiality in a second. She ordered tea in the most lovely and charming way.

Fatima returned with a tray.

'Did they bring the cake?' she asked.

'Yes.'

'What is it?'

'Cheesecake with blueberries.'

'Lovely. They're always trying to cheat me, you know . . . you can't trust them.'

She said she couldn't drink her tea when she was in bed and asked to be moved to a chair. Fatima got her up and into her chair (a long, slow process) and then, once she was in position, pulled the hem of her purple satin nightdress over her knees and down her shins. An act of gentleness and tact. My mother's phone began to ring, the trill strange and unsettling.

'That'll be the bank,' she said. 'I hate it when the bank rings. When the bank rings it means trouble. Just ignore it.' The phone rang out. She checked the screen. It had indeed been the bank. She had received cheques, she explained, over the previous few weeks and when the cheques were lodged, the exact equivalent immediately showed up as an ATM withdrawal. To the penny. This must be the reason why the bank had been ringing and had just rung.

I found this story bewildering. And alarming. Was her account being ransacked? Half-understood stories of online banking horrors I'd read over the years were at the back of my mind. I said I could check her account on her phone. Her PIN number, she told me, was 151230, her birthday. I opened the phone and went into her account but saw nothing. No cause for alarm, nothing untoward, no sign of her money being siphoned off.

Still, I said, we should ring the bank's fraud line. Yes, my wife said, we should ring the bank's fraud line. My mother would not entertain the idea. The bank people were so tiring and so wearisome, she said. We would not call the fraud line.

Yes, we should, we pressed, emphasising how easy it would be; we would do the talking but she would be on hand to verify. She wouldn't have to have anything to do with the tiring, wearisome bank people at the other end of the line. We'd take care of that part.

She refused. There was no point talking to the boring bank people, for the simple reason they didn't know anything.

But what if some scam really was underway and her account was being emptied (although the mobile app had revealed nothing)? Ringing the bank was surely the sensible thing to do? I am a practical person. My wife and I could do this.

No, she said. We will not ring the bank.

Knowing her as well as I knew her, I could recognise annoyance. Perplexed if not surprised by her refusal to act, I was even more surprised by her heat. She still had the wherewithal to take umbrage, I thought. That, at this stage, was truly astonishing.

It was time to go but the following day, I said, as we would still be in London, we would pop back at whatever time she wanted.

She said that would not work. She had no time. She could not see us.

Not even for a few minutes?

No, not even five minutes. The fact was, she said, a person was coming to help her with her book on T. S. Eliot. They were going to type up some of the text for her. Her whole day was full.

In the corridor as we made our way out, we were stopped by the senior nurse and I knew she had something she wanted us to know.

'Yesterday the hairdresser was in,' she said. 'Miss Edna said to cancel the hairdresser but I wouldn't. When the hairdresser appeared, I told her to go ahead. She went in and she did Miss Edna's hair and Miss Edna was very pleased with the result.'

She was not just delivering an anecdote, I thought; this was a message about persistence, no matter what.

The next morning I lay on my bed in Room 14 of the Chelsea Arts Club. The windows were open. It was raining in the street. I heard the tyres of the passing cars pushing through the slick of water that lay on the tarmacadam. A call came. It was my mother. Her voice was surprisingly resolute. She had recovered from the day before, she said. She had her strength back. She was very sorry about Saturday and how things ended. She had been tired, she explained. Frazzled. Not her usual self. It was the illness, she said. It was grinding her to smithereens. Would we come at six o'clock? And have a little drink?

We got to my mother's convalescent home early. My mother was out of bed and in the sitting room. She had a glass of chilled white wine in front of her. The conversation slid to the strange business with the cheques. A scam? No, and this emerged in fits and starts (and how and when this information had arrived was a mystery) but it turned out that when each lodgement was made, due to a glitch in the bank's recording system, the exact equivalent was debited. That's what had happened until the problem was eventually rectified and the sums were credited back. I was grateful for the assurance yet the nugget of fury smouldering in my gut wouldn't go away. Her fucking bank. What possessed them to act as they had? And surely, they could have come up with a better way of communicating about something that was their fault than a sequence of harrying phone calls. Capitalism has never excelled at engaging with people as they are if it means sensitivity or flexibility is required. I did know this so I ought not to have been livid at the bank's lack of care but I was.

We glided to the subject of the future. My mother said she would not be going back to Ovington Street. She could no longer live in her lovely house, either with or without care. She couldn't manage the stairs. She would have to go to a different setting, somewhere without stairs, and such a setting had been found. She was going to go to a flat a friend had offered in Belgravia. Once she got strong enough, she said, she would make the move.

For a long time, it had been obvious that the point would eventually come when she would have to give her house up and go elsewhere; and now that moment had come. The meaning with which this announcement was freighted was obvious but went unacknowledged. It could not be spoken about.

A bit later my wife commented on my mother's hair. She said how beautiful it looked. A little smile crossed my mother's face. The best part of the whole weekend.

Sometime towards the end of November, she moved into the flat in Belgravia because she couldn't go home.

On Saturday 25 November I sent my usual email asking if I could call Sunday. This exchange followed:

'. . . my phone won't work as bill unpaid! Will try and get it working tomorrow.'

'Oh Lordy. Will I try tomorrow . . .'

'You can try . . . and I will try . . .'

She succeeded with the bill-paying and the following day she rang at 6 p.m. One line of our conversation stood out and I wrote it down, it startled me so much: 'I've been in hell but I didn't die.'

After delivering that line she rung off and then a few minutes after, part of the regular pattern, she sent an email apologising for being 'dazed', which she explained was because she was 'exhausted'.

A bit later she rang for the second time that evening. She was affronted. She wanted to watch a programme about

Maria Callas but couldn't get the television to work in the flat where she was. She'd always admired Callas, of course, but this was more than a matter of being thwarted and stopped from watching a programme about an artist she venerated. With her life experience having shrunk as radically as it had the box had become one of her most consistent and important companions. To be denied this great comfort at this point in her life was an appalling loss, I thought, as I put the phone down, and I could easily see myself railing just as she had and for the same reason at some point in the not-too-distant future. At the end of life, as I knew from every old people's home I'd visited, and of which I'd just been reminded, the telly looms large.

I booked a flight to London in mid-December; this was so I could see my mother on her ninety-third birthday. I flew over the day before and when I woke the next morning in the house in Chelsea where I'd arranged to stay – it was actually in the next street to Carlyle Square where I'd lived during the 1970s in my mother's house – and I saw the light around the edge of the window blind and heard the sound of the traffic on the King's Road and footsteps on the old buckled paving stones in the street, and somebody sweeping dry, coarse leaves, using a brush with stiff bristles in a nearby garden, I recognised the light and the sounds were identical to what I would have seen and heard on waking forty-odd years ago, and with that recognition the distance between my present and my past vanished and became one.

I took myself off for breakfast. In the dining room a long table with people gathered singly or in pairs, reading their newspapers. The clack of cutlery on porcelain and the sound of the chef in the kitchen whistling listlessly. I was reminded of Patrick Hamilton's accounts of boarding-house life and the optimism I'd woken up to was banished by the exhaustion and ennui I felt in that room, lying like a blanket over everything. It was Christmas, no doubt, I decided. Christmas was only ten days away and it was always a dampener. But it couldn't just be the misery of the annual season of forced jollity. It was surely what was happening in the world and the gathering sense – and this was something I'd often heard my mother fulminate about because it had sickened her – that the old inclinations towards violence and tyranny were being embraced with unchecked enthusiasm by a new generation of reckless, shameless, strong men. It might have been ever thus but the monsters had a new spring in their step and as they rose something sank, at least in me.

After breakfast I returned to my room to work. Towards 12.30 p.m. I put on my coat and set off, not as usual for her old house in Ovington Street but her new flat in an apartment block in Belgravia. I would follow a new route but it would go through a familiar terrain. I passed cottages done up to look like Cotswold village gems, new apartment blocks for oligarchs, with porters and neatly trimmed orange trees in painted boxes at the front, mansions encrusted in stucco, thick and white like new icing, and on every building, loud and shiny and pugnacious, cameras and alarms, the paraphernalia of security. Everywhere, women in housecoats with dogs on leads staring at their phones; housekeepers who toiled in the houses round about getting ten minutes with their Instagram feed as they walked their employers' dogs. Purring by, huge cars driven by churlish men who insisted on making every pedestrian wait before crossing the road so they might take the turn and cruise on. I thought of Laius meeting Oedipus on the road to Delphi and ordering him to step off the road so his chariot could go forward. It didn't seem much had changed.

I had gifts for my mother but I stopped at a *parfumerie* which I passed on the way for one more. I bought a Verbena Vera reed diffuser (she'd had one before; she liked the scent) and as the assistant wrapped the purchase I started with the banal questions. Was Christmas a busy time? Yes. What were her clientele like? She had a few regulars whom she liked because they talked and as she was on her own all day every day she liked to talk, but for the most part the customers didn't want to talk. They just wanted to get in and get out with their purchases, quickly. And from this very modest rebuke to the people in the place to where she, an immigrant, had come to make a life, she slipped quickly but smoothly to full-scale revelation (with having little opportunity to talk she just couldn't help herself I assumed; it all just had to come out). Life in Britain, she said, for immigrants like herself was getting steadily worse. It was white people's unending, self-pity-fuelled hatred of outsiders that was to blame. The white people didn't like her because she wasn't white. Nobody who wasn't white was liked. White English people said immigrants like her were the cause of everything that was wrong with their white lives. They said it to her face. On the Tube. On the street. In the pub. Oh, yes, this was what she was hearing more and more. She was to blame. She and her kind. For everything. And the sooner she went back to wherever she came from, the better.

In the street moments later, prompted by what I'd just heard, the memory floated into my mind of Rainer Fassbinder's film *Fear Eats the Soul* (1974), which tells the story of a lonely ageing white German cleaning lady who marries a handsome, much younger black Moroccan immigrant worker; the couple, as the film charts, endure huge prejudice and antagonism because of their relationship. My mother had loved this film, as had I, and I have clear memories of our having long conversations about the iconoclastic German director's excavation of German antagonism to and prejudice against those of a different race and a different skin, attitudes excoriated in the film, which she applauded. Since then, she hadn't changed in this respect. And were I to tell her about the conversation I'd just had in the perfume shop, I thought, albeit it was unlikely I would, I could predict her reaction. She would have instinctively taken the shop assistant's side and felt outraged on her behalf. Perhaps because she'd come from Ireland (and I say 'perhaps' because I'm not sure that the argument that she felt solidarity with immigrants because she was once one herself can be made to stand up), and even though she'd had an exceptionally privileged and very white life, her gut always led her to align with the outsider who was under attack by the host because they looked different and didn't fit. Always.

I padded on, carrying my small, beautifully wrapped parcel. I passed many very thin women – armoured coats, shield-sized handbags, sunglasses worn as tiaras high on their beautiful coiffures – and workmen with dust in their eyebrows squatting on coils of cable and bags of cement outside houses under renovation (of which there were a surprising number), necking cans of Lucozade and Red Bull.

This was my first visit to where my mother had moved so everything was new. The street where she now lived was a Belgravia street; stuccoed houses and that special Belgravia atmosphere of quiet and wealth. Her block, inside which her flat was located, when it came in view wasn't a nineteenth-century icing-encrusted mansion but something twentieth century and possibly Art Deco-ish. It had unadorned walls and black, metal-framed windows. As I approached the entrance, a modest but heavy door, Bertie Wooster, who in P. G. Wodehouse's novels lives in Half Moon Street, which was not so far away, sprang to mind. Bertie W. could have happily lived here, I thought, it being close to his West End haunts. Then I remembered that the writer J. R. Ackerley, author of *My Father and Myself*, a book which had influenced me hugely, had also lived in Half Moon Street in the 1920s when he was finding his way around London. These odd conjectures were followed by a fizz of bafflement. Why was I associating what I'd already come to think of as my mother's last home with Bertie Wooster and J. R. Ackerley. What was my mind up to?

I passed through the front door and stepped into the hall. A table, a vase, flowers (artificial I guessed), tasteful modern paintings, modern lamps, nice lampshades, a muted, soothing colour scheme, carpet, marble, glass, brass; there was nothing Woosterish about the aesthetic at all. This was modern and monied. There was a desk, with a porter who smiled, said 'O'Brien?' (he'd doubtless posed the question to many people who'd floated past wanting to find their way to my mother;

this brought home that I wasn't alone in making this pilgrimage as I'd unconsciously and lazily assumed) and when I nodded, directed me to the basement.

I descended a narrow staircase, negotiated a corridor and found myself at the flat's front door. I rang the bell. The door was opened by a woman dressed in blue scrubs: she was short, spry, had an excellent smile and a smooth, unhurried, very even way of speaking. She told me her name was Beatrice and I immediately sensed two impulses were in play. On the one hand, there was propriety (she knew what needed to be said and she'd be sticking to her script; that's what she signalled); and, on the other, there was her vast empathy, which she was bursting to express (this she also signalled). My apprehension of these contradictory impulses characterised every subsequent interaction I had with every carer.

I also knew at that moment that for the immediate present propriety would prevail until we got to know each other better. After all, wasn't that the way of the world? Boundaries and protocols always trump the expression of feeling when money is in the mix and the client has the cash. In this matrix, the carer's job is to care, not be human; that would seem to be the substance of the unwritten contract, though I didn't pay much attention at the time to this revelation. Later, however, as I came to know how remarkable the carers were and how remarkable their practice was, I came to believe this cult of discretion and detachment was symptomatic of our social alienation. Why was it wrong for feelings to show, even if money was changing hands? I sometimes wondered if perhaps this rule has arisen because the clients – who are usually rich and prosperous – cannot face forming a human bond with the carers – who are usually not rich – because they fear that what they would discover, if they made friends, would discomfort them. The rich have never been very good, after all, at facing up to the difficult and even unhappy truths regarding the lives of the less fortunate. Money does have such a terrible corrosive effect on empathy. This was something I think my mother understood. The alienation between humans that wealth creates. She didn't like it either.

I entered the flat. Shiny floors and newly painted doors. My mother was in a room off the kitchen. An untouched open sandwich on the slate table in front of her: white bread, Gorgonzola Dolce and slivers of pale smoked salmon with lemon juice and pepper. The smell of the lemon and the pepper and the fish, mild and comforting. Her tiny, creased hand when I shook it was like a piece of origami; a small, weightless, perfect representation of a small creature folded tight around itself. She said she hoped, it being her birthday, I hadn't brought any presents. She'd been delivering this line on her birthday for years, for decades even, and she always said it in the same way. A mix of the arch and the mischievous. However, she didn't literally mean it. (Were the gifts to stop coming she wouldn't have been happy.) Saying she wanted no gifts was a schtick she habitually deployed and which she knew, from experience, when thrown out or down, always had a powerful effect. Whoever heard her say it for the first time was always bumped into a new state of being because the admonishment was so unusual, so startling. It was one way (and a very important way) by which she created her mystique.

I presented my gifts: hand cream, a purple shawl and the fragrance diffuser from the *parfumerie*. I was told I shouldn't. That was also part of her spiel. Beatrice brought me tea and biscuits and cheese. I ate but she just looked at her food and talked, not attempting a coherent argument but just letting the statements come, one after the next, about how terrible it was to be sick and how she would not wish it on anyone and how, when one was sick and old, it was literally impossible to get help. It was her fate, she said – she was now warming to her theme – to be endlessly, eternally let down. Doctors were the worst. Now she abruptly changed tack. She had thought, she said, she was getting better in the hospital. Then she came here to this flat. And what did she find? she asked rhetorically. She found she should've stayed in the hospital, where she was getting better. That's what she found. In the hospital recovery was theoretically possible at least. But not here. Why was that? Simple. Here she was at everyone's mercy. All day, every day, the emails flooded in. Why did no one understand what it was to be sick? Well, that's what people were like. They didn't understand. So, they sent their emails and every email was asinine and stupid and moronic and every email had to be answered and she could hardly see, and she was not getting on with her book . . .

This was a human being at the end of their tether. It was hard but necessary to hear. The slide towards extinction was not the slide towards the sleep of tradition, an idea to which we are all under enormous social pressure to subscribe. Death, say the advocates of this nostrum – should you challenge them – is so hideous we shouldn't make it worse by being honest about it. Let its horrors be horrors briefly glimpsed after a life of blissful ignorance at the very end and not for very long, just before death. My mother, predictably I have to say, was having none of that. She would testify to the brutal truth and she did and terrible as it was to hear, it was also bracing. She wouldn't baulk; she would resist; she would cavil. Wasn't that the better way to face extinction, to say loudly over and over and over, 'No, no, no, it's hideous'?

'You've come all this way to see me,' she said. 'It must've cost you a great deal of money and a great deal of time and a great deal of effort.'

I protested it hadn't.

'Yes, yes, it must have, and I hardly think it was worth your while. I'm afraid I don't amount to much.'

I demurred again.

'I don't amount to much and actually, if truth be told, it was completely pointless your coming, really.'

I was happy to have come, I said. It was worth the effort.

There was nothing more to say, she said, with finality.

I said we could just sit in silence. That would be lovely.

And we did. We sat. Beatrice moved in and out of the kitchen and through the room and out to the other rooms in the flat several times. Once she passed carrying a bundle of laundry, freshly laundered and smelling delicious. My mother touched her plate now and again and eventually broke off a tiny piece of cheese, which she put into her mouth and ate very slowly. I finished my tea. I made myself a second cup. Beatrice turned on the hoover in the bedroom. The sound was low and soothing. I've always liked hoovers whirring in the distance. My second cup finished, I poured a third and drank it. Time passed. Sometimes I caught my mother's eye and she saw me and sometimes when I caught her eye I saw she wasn't seeing me; she was seeing something else. The emerald coast perhaps? I didn't ask.

The bell went. She rolled her eyes.

'Do you see what I mean?' she said. 'It's never quiet, it's never still. There's no tranquillity. It's just like this all day, every day, people here, people there, demanding, demanding, demanding, coming, coming, coming, it's exhausting, exhausting, exhausting.' The triple-triplet utterance – a venerable linguistic conceit of hers.

The visitor entered; tall, female, her face covered with a mask, a wedding ring flashing on her wedding finger; she was laden with boxes. Her words tumbled forth; the mask was a precaution, she explained, not an indicator of there being anything wrong. But the last thing she wanted was to make my mother sick if she was carrying a bug but didn't know she was. Especially not today of all days, my mother's ninety-third birthday. Oh, what an age Edna had reached, she continued, her tone warm and enthusiastic and lovely. And now we were going to celebrate and it would be splendid and joyful. 'And,' she concluded, 'your son is here, Edna. Isn't that wonderful?'

The visitor opened a box and produced a magnificent and extravagant birthday cake. My mother grimaced.

'Will you have a slice of birthday cake?' said the visitor.

No, my mother said quietly but very clearly. Absolutely not. She asked for the cake to be put away in the refrigerator in the kitchen. The cake was carried off. From the kitchen, the sounds of light clatter as the fridge was reorganised and space for the cake was made. 'There'll be no cake today, you understand,' my mother whispered to me, '*No* cake.'

The visitor returned and from another bag produced a bottle of champagne. A sheen of condensation on the glass. It had been brought chilled. It was ready to drink. What about a glass?

No, my mother said again quietly but very clearly. Absolutely not. The champagne was to follow the cake and go in the refrigerator too. The visitor went back to the kitchen. More sounds of light clatter as space for the champagne was made.

'There'll be no champagne today, you understand,' my mother whispered. '*No* champagne.'

The visitor returned, undaunted and still ebullient. It was present time, she announced, delightedly. She moved the smoked salmon plate and set a very large and beautifully wrapped box in front of my mother.

'What's this?' asked my mother.

A present of course, the visitor explained, from a friend.

The parcel was opened and out of it was pulled a woollen fawn skirt and a sky-blue housecoat.

Fawn, my mother said, eying the skirt, was a dreary colour worn by dreary women.

The visitor said she could take the skirt back to Harrods and change it. The receipt was in the bag. That would be easy. What colour would my mother like?

Black, my mother said. Obviously, black. The blue house coat she would keep. It might do.

*

The visitor left and an enormously tall man, he was six foot six at least, loped in; he was named Clyde. He wore a track-suit and old espadrilles with their heels worn down and no socks. Clyde approached my mother. Clyde was a chef and he had cooked for her in the past. He had brought gifts, he said, in his rich Afrikaans accent, and showed them balanced on his spade-sized palms: a couple of little ramekins with what looked like a firm, pale custard and a vitrine with berries to sprinkle on the custard.

It's the vanilla-flavoured panna cotta you love, he said; the one I always made you. Her favourite panna cotta on her birthday. Would she have one?

No, my mother said. Absolutely not. She instructed Clyde to put the panna cotta and the berries away in the refrigerator. Clyde went off to the kitchen. Sounds as space for the ramekins of panna cotta and the vitrine of berries were made.

'There'll be *no* panna cotta today,' my mother whispered. 'Nor berries. Not today. Not any day.'

Clyde left. My mother spoke:

'Do you see what it's like here? All these people coming with their different demands . . . I'm sick and I'm in pain. A doctor was meant to come but didn't. That's how it is. Nobody will help you anymore. Nobody. You're on your own. I should've stayed in the hospital. I was getting better in the hospital. Now I'm here and I'm not getting better. No, I'm getting worse. I'm getting worse now I'm here . . . I just want to go to bed and lie down. I want to lie down forever. And you've come all the way . . . from Ireland. When did you come? Did you come yesterday or today? You came yesterday, I see. What a long way you came, and I'm sorry to say, I don't think it was worth your while. You can hear my voice is fading. My strength is going. I usually have a sleep in the afternoon. And I'm going to have to have a sleep very shortly. I know you have come a long way but I'm afraid you must go now because I am afraid if I don't lie down, I will fall over. That's what you fear more than anything at this stage. You fear that you will stand and fall. To fall is the worst thing, absolutely the worst thing. You absolutely do not want to fall. You fall; you don't get up. I have help and I should be grateful but I don't know any more about anything. I'm so tired, so tired.'

I put on my coat and hat. My mother asked me to kiss her on the top of her head. As I did, she put up her spindly right hand and gently stroked my left cheek. Then she took my hand and kissed it.

When I got outside it was dusk, the special December dusk of London. Four middle-aged white blokes on a jolly staggered by. I didn't quite know what I was feeling but I knew if I waited, I would find out. The psyche always offers an explanation in the end.

I began the walk back to the house where I was staying. The paving stones underfoot were lovely worn slabs with dips in them like old butchers' chopping boards.

I passed a couple dressed identically in blue woollen coats and jaunty baseball caps worn back to front with writing on them, 'His' and 'Hers'.

The shops in Walton Street all had their lights on and some had their doors open and as I passed, I could feel the heat from inside coming out.

Ten minutes had passed and now I began to grasp what exactly was swirling within; it was not only my mother's looming death which was weighing on me; it was also the decline of the place where she'd lived and to which she had committed herself for the bulk of her life.

When we had arrived in London from Dublin half a century and more ago, the British political class had competence; even the Tory ones had competence; but now the country was run by a confederacy of incompetent, corrupt, hard-right, anti-European, xenophobic, racist, Brexit-obsessed Tory scoundrels, men and women with hard hearts, no empathy and no capacity for self-reflection. Gripped by the conviction that everything they achieved was down to their own industry and having no sense of the advantages that flowed from being members of their caste and class, this cohort had a limitless sense of their own entitlement and fitness to rule. They were careless and cruel and utterly unable to comprehend the harms they had wrought. The catastrophe had appalled as well as desolated my mother and she had vehemently denounced those she identified as at fault in many of her final conversations and I did feel sorry that she had had to see this. But my feelings at this moment were less to do with her and more to do with me. What had happened, I now realised, was that in my mind, my mother's and Britain's decline had elided, and the grief I felt over the one fed into the grief I felt over the other and vice versa. Magical thinking is the belief that one's thoughts, actions or rituals can directly influence external events even without a logical or causal connection and what I was feeling was a variant of that tradition. Magical conjunction perhaps, with simultaneous phenomena of decline joining together to produce an effect of maximum desolation. It was something I believe my mother would have understood since she also saw all too clearly how the place where she'd lived most of her life had lost its way.

I had just come back to the room where I was staying when an email from her arrived (of course, what else?); 'I was barely able to move. I am deeply sorry . . .' she wrote. The next day another arrived in which she thanked me for the 'precious gifts' (the vital importance of the thank-you letter, which had been drummed into me in childhood, was still, despite everything, also part of her own regime) and added, referring to the visit, 'Sorry I was in bad shape but hoping [I] get better . . .'

I went back to Ireland. Two days before Christmas her carer sent a text from her phone. My mother had deleted her email app by mistake and could not send or receive emails. She hoped to find someone to fix it and would then be in touch.

By New Year's Eve she was back online. I rang her. I couldn't get through. She rang me back. Normal pleasantries to start but then she segued to her ill health. She had thought she was improving, and on the mend, she said, and so she'd gone to a friend's for Christmas lunch. A misjudgement. During the meal she started to feel unwell. She had to leave and come home. The blasted illness was remorseless. It had felled her and it wouldn't stop until she was done for. (This was what she said, not 'died'.) Why had no one warned her what to expect? (This dereliction she found particularly egregious, hence she couldn't stop repeating it.) She was in a bad place. Her body was failing. Failing . . . If only she could finish the blasted Eliot book. She was trying to write. Trying. But it was so hard. Her eyes were hopeless. Everything was hopeless. It was all so hard. When was I coming to see her?

Sometime in January or early February, I said.

'Would . . .' and here she stumbled. 'Would your wife . . . what is her name?' she said.

My stomach (the body reacting faster than the mind) curdled at the question, which I had never expected her to ask. My father's forgetfulness when he was in a home in Dublin and dementia was washing through him, I had accepted reluctantly; but my mother's forgetfulness was something I did not wish to encounter and I was not prepared to countenance.

I told her. Tyga.

'Yes, will she come too?'

'We'll both come but we'll come separately and we'll both see you.'

'I have to stop now,' she said. 'I can't talk for long anymore. This wretched illness, it's done me down, laid me low. I haven't the strength any more to do much of anything . . . I'll say goodbye . . .'

A bit later came a message, the punctuation and spelling of which told me it was written by the carer: 'I am sorry not to chat but the truth is I am in a bad way at this time.'

2024

My journal entry written on New Year's Day was three lines long: 'Another year. I don't know what I feel. I am awaiting a signal from within.'

At the end of the week of the new year, I was working at my computer when a notification appeared. I was surprised to see my mother's name and number; there was a FaceTime call coming through from her, the first she'd ever placed. I accepted the call and her image appeared on my screen. She was sitting at the table in the kitchen in her new flat, in the same place with the same posture with her back not touching the seat's back as when I had visited on her birthday.

'Hello,' I said, 'it's me.'

I was not who she expected to see. Her face said so and then her words confirmed this. She'd been trying to ring someone else (she didn't say who), she explained, but she'd pressed not their number but mine, and now here I was, and now here she was. She apologised for disturbing me. I said she'd nothing to worry about on that score. I was hoping a conversation might follow but was soon disabused of this notion. She must call the person she had been trying to call, she said, and she must go. Yes, yes, I thought. As I knew perfectly well, she was always an absolutist when it came to the diary and her tasks. She wasn't going to deviate off course because she'd accidentally pressed the wrong number. I have the same inherited inclination myself. I don't veer and I don't embrace the accidental, or happenstance. Our non-encounter reminded me of how alike we were.

Later it occurred to me that rather than speaking on the phone we could talk on FaceTime. It would be better than the phone.

I sent an email that said, 'Shall I call you on FaceTime tomorrow?'

The next day at about 8 p.m. I received an email from my mother's account. Written by the carer. My mother was 'not at all well' and was 'trying to get a doctor to come to the house as her illness has got worse'. I wondered if it was the doctor she'd been trying to contact when she accidently called me on FaceTime. I would never know. The carer signed off, 'Please excuse her for being unable to be in touch; a broken phone is adding to the problem.'

I now found myself brooding on the FaceTime incident. The person whose face I'd accidently seen was clearly involved in the struggle to stay alive. What was I doing badgering her with requests? Our contacts might make me feel better but what benefit were they to her? None. They just sapped scarce energy and she needed to husband all she had and devote it to staying alive. In the light of which, I decided, for the time being, I wouldn't bother her. If she wanted, she'd be in touch, if not no matter. She needed to focus on what was paramount.

That Sunday, the first of the year and our traditional talking day, I heard nothing. I'd made my mind up. I would hold back and not oblige her to use up valuable energy dealing with me. But, of course, a virtuous position, which is fine and dandy in principle, still leaves one with anxieties and doubts and questions. The body has its own response system, which is absolutely beyond the mind's control. I couldn't turn off my visceral need to know. I had to know. However, I couldn't write to her so I wrote to the carer instead. She was on the ground. She could tell me what was happening. And she did. She told me by return that my mother was unwell though getting better. It was a calming report. Short, not too much detail, soothing. Brevity at its best.

The following Sunday, 14 January, there was no word from my mother but again I resisted calling; if she was still unwell, she wouldn't want to be bothered. I just had to wait till she was ready. I was right.

The next day, Monday, she wrote, and everything was explained. On Saturday, she'd fallen – 'This happened in my sleep almost' was her cryptic description – and so on Sunday, she'd been 'unable to function', which was why I hadn't heard from her. The information was troubling. I actually knew of someone who had fallen out of bed while asleep and died; tumbling from bed to one's death was a real thing: but aside from its truth as something that could happen, it also had a separate meaning for me. It confirmed I'd been right to hang back. Again, I reminded myself, though I might want to talk, I had to remember she often didn't and it was nothing to do with me; she simply hadn't the space. In her incredibly diminished life – perhaps the kind I one day would end up living, perhaps the kind we all one day end up living – what could be accommodated was strictly limited; in her case, she could do nothing else but what was keeping her alive.

Oh, what a finagling business was communicating – but now I knew what to do; stay quiet! I did all week but eventually the point arrived when I couldn't not ring. I dialled the following Friday, 19 January, at six in the evening, when I guessed she might be having a drink and would welcome a chat. She answered. She was frazzled, angry. She complained she was at the mercy of doctors (she had five physicians, she said) and one was charging £7,000 to make a home visit. I knew better than to query the figure. I regretted that I hadn't stuck to my plan. I rung off. In less than a minute she rang back. The doctor was charging £700 a visit, she said. I was astounded. Harried though she was she remained vigilant and when she knew she was wrong she was quick to correct herself.

Here was something to welcome. And we were talking.

My wife was nearby. I turned on the speaker and now they spoke.

My wife asked where she was.

My mother answered she was in bed.

And how was she? asked my wife.

She was too tired to answer questions, my mother said. Yet not seemingly to talk. She repeated what I had heard her say before. And the more she talked the more it was borne in on me: the book on T. S. Eliot, *The Hermit Thrush*, that she was desperate to finish, was not just a literary artefact which she must complete because that's what writers did; they got their books finished because that was their duty. It was an elixir of life, her elixir of life.

On the evening of Sunday 21 January, Storm Isha landed. The wind was hard. It hurled stuff against the windows and wrenched the schoolhouse about, threatening, I felt, to rip it off its foundations and hurl it into the air. My wife made me move away from the windows in case the glass shattered and I was showered with shards. I'd never done anything like this during the three decades I'd lived there; but then I'd never known a storm like Isha before. Another sign of a world out of joint.

In bed sleep was impossible at first until, sometime in the early morning, the wind dropped, the house stopped shaking and away I drifted . . . When I woke it was light and my first thought was of my mother. I was slightly nettled. Couldn't my psyche have dropped its preternatural hyper-vigilance just for once and let me worry about the schoolhouse roof or the trees in the garden for a change? No, it couldn't. Day after week after month, the mind never missed the opportunity to crash in with its usual warning: 'Today might be the day, and if it is, are you ready?' Even Storm Isha couldn't stop it doing that. Yet I wished the storm had. I wanted a day off from the incessant alarms; I wanted a rest; I wanted to forget. So: ruthless truth-telling on the one hand and the longing for denial on the other – the two contradictory impulses operating in perfect harmony in the same mind simultaneously, and without either cutting the other off. What a curious organ the psyche was.

A week later, on Monday 29 January, I rang my mother and got through. Immediately. The voice was still faint and etiolated but it had a new drive.

'Thank goodness the weather has turned,' she began. 'It is so warm here in London now. Almost balmy. Today and yesterday as well . . . It's very difficult, I'm in a wheelchair now, I can't get around, I'm dependent on everyone if I need to get anywhere . . . Anyway, there's a little bit of outside here . . . It's a yard really but it's outside and yesterday and today I sat out there . . . Beatrice wheeled me out . . . and there was the sun and the sky and the clouds and I said to Beatrice, whom I love, I said, "Beatrice, I'd like to be alone for a while," and Beatrice, she completely understood and she left me and I sat there, yesterday and again today, both of them lovely clear balmy days like we haven't seen here for a while . . . I hadn't had the experience of being out in nature since I don't know when, since I went to hospital, and it had such an effect on me to be out in the air . . . We forget how important it is to be out in the fresh air . . . It restored my sight, it restored my hope, it restored everything . . . I was utterly transformed and I can now say that on account of that change, *I will finish Eliot* . . . I haven't said it before and this is the first time I've been able to say it . . . I can, *I will finish Eliot* . . . It won't be the shimmering beauty I had hoped it would be, alas, oh no, not that, but it will be clear and clean and comprehensible, and all thanks to the open air, the sun, the sky, and the clouds . . . We forget how important they are and what the consequences of separation from nature are . . . They're terrible, they're deathly, the consequences of separation . . . But I am so much better . . . I expect to live to ninety-four, yes, I will be ninety-four this year . . . I expect to live and I will finish Eliot . . . I think of you, you know . . . I think of you all leading your lives . . . I think about so many things . . . I'm thinking of course, besides of you, about people, about the titans, Beethoven for instance . . . what a genius, colossal, he understood so much, maybe everything . . . And if I have a regret about my life, it's this . . . I didn't get across the other arts; I didn't get across music or painting or dance . . . I was obsessed, just obsessed with literature and as a result I missed out on so much . . . I regret that . . . If I had my life over again, I'd try to rectify that . . . Of course, such wishes, they're foolish . . . You don't live your life again . . . no, no . . . Oh little did I know the day would come when I'd have to face it . . . I am facing it . . . I have faced it . . . I know what's coming . . . I know I'm going to die . . . My poor mother . . . I think of her facing it . . . Terrified . . . My poor father also . . . He was high-hearted the day he was dying . . . It was his birthday . . . He was in that nursing home in Clare, in Newmarket-on-Fergus was it? . . . I sent flowers, not that I loved him very much, that day he was dying, and I heard, they told me, someone told me, that on that actual day, the day he was dying, he was over the moon. He couldn't have been happier . . . Dying, dying, it's not easy you know . . . My pain, the pain, is terrible, it's terrible . . . But the despair has lessened, the despair has lifted . . . It was sitting outside in the air that did that . . . But the last while, the last few months, they have been terrible . . . I couldn't do anything . . . And all these people I know, they all wrote to me . . . Why can you not see us? they wrote . . . They wanted to know what they'd done . . . But they hadn't done anything . . . They'd done nothing . . . I simply hadn't the energy; I couldn't even pick up a spoon let alone phone or text . . . I could do literally nothing . . . But now, now . . . you're going to yoga now . . . is that true? I hope it's disciplined and concentrated . . . And you have a job at Trinity? . . . A miracle . . . I don't drink anymore you know . . . Life has changed and it will go on changing . . .'

I noted all this down immediately after we finished talking.

On the first Sunday of February we spoke as usual; the second Sunday of February when I rang, I got no answer. I sent an email: '. . . tried just now . . . when is a good time to call . . .?'

Beatrice replied instantly. My mother was 'sick and sleepy'; she sent love and would call soon.

I wrote in my diary, 'the uncertainty and the volatility of her situation is exhausting'.

The next Saturday, 17 February, my mother rang. She was incensed by events in Russia and America that were happening in parallel: the death of the dissident Alexei Navalny and the establishment by Donald Trump of a fighting fund to which he was asking MAGA supporters to donate so he could settle what the courts had insisted he must pay. Here, she said, was a perfect example of the world's dysfunction: on the one hand, a good man murdered in prison on the orders of the tyrant president Putin, and on the other, the American tyrant, who'd been found guilty, not only not going to jail, but getting his supporters to pay his fines. From here it was on to the 'bloody book' she had to finish and the dereliction of others who'd failed to warn her 'about old age' and the body's failing and the cancer that had dogged her for years and how difficult it was for her to write and then to revise what she had written and then her talk took a truly extraordinary tack:

'I hardly go out, it's so difficult,' she said, 'but last week I went to the Palace, Kensington Palace . . . The Queen was doing something for the Dames and I am one and she wanted to be photographed with me but I went in a wheelchair and I couldn't be got up the stairs so we couldn't do the photograph . . . I like her, the Queen, I admire her, and I know her, she's a woman of integrity . . . But the event was a huge effort for me and the guests all talking and making out they were so happy and so pleased to be there and it was all utterly false, utterly false the way they were acting . . . They weren't expressing real sincere feelings . . . That happens a lot I find nowadays . . . There's so much falseness . . . but I went and I made it through though it took a lot out of me . . . I was exhausted for days afterwards . . .'

Looking back through my diaries and re-reading this entry, I do wonder if this was the last social engagement of her life.

Over the next four weeks I received one bleak email or text after another either from her or Beatrice: she was sick, she was in hospital, she was home again but too tired to talk. We finally spoke on 17 March. She was incensed. It was the BBC. Their St Patrick's Day coverage was woeful and why was there no mention of the Pogues' singer Shane MacGowan, who'd recently died? I was unsurprised (BBC dereliction always infuriated her inner patriot) yet amazed she still had the ability to be so angry.

We now entered the period of accelerating decline: increasingly she would fall ill, run a fever and suffer an infection requiring antibiotics, needing to sleep and sometimes needing to go to hospital; and then she would return from hospital and require more sleep. Reading over my journals, which cover this period, I find my entries were either brusque recapitulations of what happened – 'She doesn't really want to see anybody (nobody other than doctors) but she likes texts and telephone calls when she's strong enough to receive them' – or short iterations of foreboding – 'It is a very fraught, long drawn-out process . . . Though I could be wrong, I think it will not be long.'

But now and again she was restored to herself (I thought of this as like a pendulum swinging back except of course as an analogy this was incorrect: a pendulum is regular whereas these interludes were irregular and erratic) and at these times she would talk vividly and eloquently about the world. Her political ire was undimmed. She loathed Trump and dreaded his victory over Biden in the forthcoming presidential election. She was deeply exercised by the sufferings of the Ukrainians and the Palestinians. She hated Putin and the Russian army, and she hated Netanyahu and the Israeli Defense Forces. I was moved by her sympathy, as well as amazed she still had the strength to fulminate as she did. But I was also troubled by the unwelcome thought which came floating in – death would spare her from having to endure the further horrors that are coming. This was nonsense: she didn't want to die; she wanted to recover and to go on writing. I knew this yet still the thought of what she would escape by dying kept needling, like a drunk who won't shut up.

At the end of March, another stage on the descending path: as there was no likelihood of her ever returning, it was decided her house in Ovington Street should be cleared and the keys returned to the landlord. My wife agreed to go to London with my youngest son to do this fiendish job while I would stay in Ireland. I had just been commissioned to make a podcast for the BBC on the 1983 Maze escape, when dozens of IRA men got out of what was supposedly the world's most secure prison, and this had to be written, ten fourteen-minute episodes in two or so months.

The second Saturday of May; I rang my mother.

'How are you?'

'Not good. Very bad. Very bad.'

'. . .'

'And I'm trying to do the impossible.'

The above was followed by a few more remarks (my son, now in London with my wife and clearing her house, was coming to see her Sunday, she was very tired, she didn't know if she'd get *The Hermit Thrush* over the line). Then she said she was too tired to talk anymore and that was the end of the call.

For the rest of May and throughout June all our conversations were essentially a repeat of this one. Politics and the sufferings of human beings were never mentioned now.

On 6 July, the first Sunday of the month, Beatrice sent me a long medical bulletin with the heading 'Updates with Mrs Edna O'Brien'. Her mobility was 'quite poor'; her coordination 'not good'; she declined food if asked so had to be fed all the time; she was 'responsive to questions' and 'with it at times' but otherwise sleepy and drowsy; she was short of breath; she was restless all the previous night 'wanting to get out of bed every 30 minutes . . . more or less' and at 5 a.m. she injured her shin on the bed rail (sterile strips and a bandage were required to stop the bleeding) before finally going to sleep at 8.15. A few minutes after sending this, Beatrice sent a second message saying her last message had been meant for the doctor and then she rang. Your mother is sick, she said. Her message and its implication were blunt but her voice was even and calm. The way she inflected the word sick made me ask the question. Is she about to die? I asked. Beatrice knew I'd booked flights and was coming on 22 July but I wanted to know – should I come earlier? Beatrice refused to be drawn; she said it was up to me. But I thought the implication was obvious. After the call finished, I booked tickets for two days hence, Tuesday 9 July. I would go over first thing in the morning and come back on the last flight in the evening.

After I booked the flights and prompted by my feeling of there being a change in my mother for the worse, I felt compelled to dig out and re-read a letter that my father had written in December 1956 describing his mother, my grandmother, Margaret (Rita) Gébler's, death. And having re-read the letter I found myself 'remembering' the events he described, the pictures I saw being tricked up by my imagination using details taken from my father's words, though of course I couldn't have 'seen' what I remembered because I hadn't been present.

I see a room in the Richmond Hospital in Dublin, a turf fire burning in the open grate, and Rita, tiny and fragile, lying dying in the bed.

I see her corpse on the mortuary table under a shroud with my mother and father standing close by. They each touch the face, 'soft to the touch as a baby's [skin], and icy cold', as my father wrote.

I see my parents, moving along the frozen quays as they made their way home from the morgue in the early morning to the Dublin suburb where we lived, a full moon in the sky, the Liffey's surface all rosy from the Christmas lights strung across the bridges, the bells of Christ Church chiming in the distance as the bell-ringers practised 'Good King Wenceslas'.

The experience of the last few years had prompted memories but never had I known anything like this where something was entirely made up. It was the mind's way of putting me on warning, I decided. It was about to happen.

On Tuesday 9 July I was due to fly out of Belfast International Airport at 6 a.m. To clear security, I had to be at the airport by 4.30 a.m. at the latest. And to be there at 4.30 a.m., I had to get up at 2 a.m., and when I did, I found a message on my phone. Beatrice had written it just before midnight, when she was about to go home, having finished her shift, and when it pinged in, I had been asleep. This was why I only found it when I got up. 'Hi Carlo,' it ran, 'your mum suddenly has recovered just today late afternoon almost like her old self. To think that she has been poorly for a couple of weeks and semi-unconscious for the last two days. She really is a fighter. Safe travels . . .' (Beatrice I knew would not be there when I got to London; it would be Amelia.)

I dressed and went and stood at my front gate with my coat and bag. The night was very black. There was no moon. The air was moist, even balmy. Nothing stirring, no sound of any kind. Then far away, the sound of a car, a diesel, and then its headlights needling down Macaulay's hill. I had decided not to drive and this was my transport to the airport. The driver pulled up and I got in and off we went along a succession of narrow empty roads. For ninety minutes there was nothing to see in the sky and then, their appearance magical as well as sudden, great splashes of pink and yellow appeared in the east on the horizon.

I got to Belfast International Airport at about 4 a.m. Departures was bunged. Hen parties (one group in denim minis and cowboy hats bar the bride who was in a grass skirt and a veil). Solitary men (factory workers or security guards returning to their hard-scrabble lives in Dagenham or Northolt). Holidaymakers in shorts, flip-flops, Crocs, sundresses, tank tops, hats, sunglasses, ready for the Mediterranean beaches where they would be sunning themselves by noon. Everyone downing pints and spritzers and rum-and-Cokes, with more pints and spritzers and rum-and-Cokes waiting on the tables before them so they wouldn't have to queue. The atmosphere febrile, skittish, edgy. Something could kick off.

The sights released my inner Savonarola, a zealot who wants everyone to take to heart the knowledge that they are going to die and live accordingly. 'You are all mortal,' I wanted to shout. 'Instead of getting sloshed, why not face that truth?'

I bought a bowl of porridge and a croissant and found a place at a table with an elderly couple. They talked to me giddily though neither were drinking. She was a seamstress and she lamented the diminishment of dressmaking skills amongst girls. Not even her grandchildren, she said, wanted to learn how to sew on a button. And yet, as she could testify, dressmaking – she'd been a dressmaker all her life – had provided her with fifty years and rising of employment. (My inner Savonarola loved this bit.) Her home place was Bangor on the east coast of Northern Ireland; in her and her husband's opinion, boisterously asserted, Bangor was a kip from which they took every opportunity they could to skedaddle; they were about to jet off to Ibiza and then they were having a week's cruise to Gibraltar; they also had their Christmas holiday planned – Tenerife. 'We both love lazing around,' the seamstress announced, defiantly. 'There are no flies on us. Try and catch us if you can but you won't. We'll be gone. We'll have flown.'

A packed plane. The man beside me had a wracking cough. With each convulsion he splattered phlegm onto a handkerchief and exclaimed, 'Dirty, dirty.'

We landed at Gatwick in good time but then sat on the runway. No steps were available. When I finally got inside, the terminus was frenzied and humid. As I walked towards the train, it was easy to imagine I was in the opening shots of a dystopian film about the collapse of civilisation. This always happens at Gatwick.

Like the plane, the train was jammed. As it chugged towards Victoria, I sat staring out the window. I had occasional distant views of the swelling Downs, but mostly what I saw – and it was thanks to Labour Party politicians who were struggling with where to build more houses that this word had recently entered my vocabulary – mostly what I saw was grey belt. Some sections were littered with railway detritus (track, sleepers, ballast, rusting carriages) and some with abandoned factories (sagging roofs, fallen gutters, broken windows, parking lots with burnt-out cars). Here and there were lovely old houses, and even lovelier farmhouses with gardens and small orchards. As always, I wondered how this higgledy-piggledy pattern had arisen.

Closer to London, the grey belt gave away to suburbia. We passed through Purley where my mother often took me as an adolescent on Sundays to visit the actress Angharad Rees (blonde, full of mirth) at her parents' house (her father, William, was a psychiatrist, her mother, Catherine, was a gentle, lovely woman who didn't ignore me as adults often tended to do). We always went on Sundays and we would always sit out in the Reeses' large and very beautiful garden and William would talk about psychiatry. Though I'd passed through Purley many times going backwards and forwards to Gatwick over the years, I hadn't thought about those visits for fifty years. And now I had. Of course, I knew why. The mind was up to its usual tricks, gleaning every mother-associated memory shard it could lay hands on and offering it up for my delectation.

Then it was on through Croydon and then beyond Croydon, south London, terraces of brick-built houses and, at least for me who had lived in south London in childhood, a haunting atmosphere of melancholy.

*

Eventually, Victoria Station; in childhood it was the cavernous and echoey location of the Cartoon Cinema, where my mother regularly brought my brother and I during the unhappy years in the early 1960s after she and my father separated but before she got custody; she would also take us to the News Cinema at Waterloo. She would only have us for a few hours (it was all my father would allow) and we would sit in the dark in the Cartoon Cinema (or the News Cinema) for the afternoon, watching the programme as it repeated, and while we did my mother would cry, quietly, decorously, and I would sit watching the screen, unable to experience any pleasure, though I knew I should. I loved cartoons, I was mad for cartoons. However, so colossal was my dread of what I knew was coming (our return home), I would always find myself wishing this time in the cinema could just be over, and I could just be back at 257 Cannon Hill Lane, immediately. The pain of separation *after* it had happened was far easier to bear than when I was waiting, knowing it was looming.

Since those dismal afternoons I have been in Victoria many times, but I have never liked it. (The same is true of Waterloo.) Even today, with not only the cinema gone (just as at Waterloo) but everything changed from what it had been like in childhood – it was now a sprawling shopping emporium with white walls and white floors and was flooded with prosperous passengers with their coffees and their baked goods in see-through cellophane envelopes rushing for their trains – the feelings nagged. Some places are forever contaminated, it seems.

I took the Tube (Victoria line) to Green Park; the carriage was grubby, muggy. At Green Park I wandered through a labyrinth of sweaty tunnels to the Piccadilly line where I caught a westbound train to Hyde Park Corner. Here I got out and found myself in the familiar warren of rank underpasses by which I would get up to the street. Here and there on the ground, at what I guessed were the premier busking and rough sleeping spots, small grey pillows had been laid out on the floor by the homeless in much the same way as a holidaymaker might secure a spot on a beach or a lounger by leaving their towel, their paperback and their sun cream. Over the years of living in and then visiting London, I have never not been aware of the homeless and the suffering poor, but the closer to the present I am, the more present they are. It was the same with my mother; she spoke of the homeless too, endlessly, albeit – unlike me, which makes it more striking – she rarely if ever used public transport and always went by taxi or minicab. How did she see the signs since she wasn't in the streets? I don't know but she did.

*

Above ground I nipped down Belgrave Place and headed for Grosvenor Square. Mansions, embassies, big houses. Expensive cars, many driven by someone in livery. Rubbish-free gutters and impeccable, chewing-gum-and-splatter-free paving stones.

Inside my mother's block I glided by the table, vase, artificial flowers, modern paintings, modern lamps, nice lampshades, all of which I'd become familiar with from previous visits, and everything I'd been feeling up till now, all the numerous disgruntlements that had jabbed at me since I started the journey at my gate in Fermanagh in the dark, vanished in a blink and in their place came a sense of calmness and even cheerfulness. Throughout my life it has always happened this way: the unknown, at first unfamiliar (like this building, like this hallway) becomes familiar, and once we are knitted together and we have become familiar, the known space can work magic on me and restore me to my factory settings so to speak, even if it's a place where I know only bad or sad things have and will happen.

I reached the front door of my mother's flat and rang the bell and Amelia (who worked with Beatrice) opened the door. She stepped back and invited me in.

I slipped across the threshold into a narrow chamber connecting my mother's bedroom and the kitchen and immediately heard, coming from my left, my mother's laboured breathing as she lay stretched on her hospital bed and the amplified sound of her breathing coming through the monitor in the kitchen. There was a slight delay and the sounds were out of sync but overlaid. The combination – the human sound and the same sound delayed – was terrifying yet weirdly aesthetic, like something in a gallery exhibiting a conceptual art sound piece about culmination.

Amelia asked me to wait while she and a new addition, a nurse, Veronica, attended to my mother. I lurked in the kitchen and made myself a cup of tea. My phone rang. It was the producer of the series and podcast *Escape from the Maze* that I'd just recorded and which was about to air on BBC Radio 4. BBC management had just ruled, he explained. They needed a line at the top of each episode: 'This podcast contains descriptions of extreme violence.'

The line could be delivered, he continued, by the continuity announcer who would tell listeners this as the programme was about to air. Or it could be me who said it, inside the body of each episode. He thought that was the better option. I didn't see anything wrong with that. Great, he said. Could I record the line on my phone and ping it to Belfast? Okay, I said. And could I do it, like, now? he said.

I went to the sitting room at the other end of the flat and closed the heavy door. I could still just hear my mother's breathing amplified by the speaker. I sat down at my mother's desk in her orthopaedic chair. On the desktop, the yellow notepads she favoured and her favourite violet-coloured pens in a jug. I leant my iPhone against the jug. I pressed record and spoke the line, 'This podcast contains descriptions of extreme violence' quickly, slowly, blandly, authoritatively, casually, moodily, forcefully, coolly, wisely, frankly, sternly, fervently, ardently, warmly, enthusiastically, and as I did I felt both self-conscious *and* un-self-conscious. On the one hand, this moment felt like something in a play or a film or a story – all the different versions and the sawing breath, faint but unmissable in the background. On the other hand, it felt like nothing; I was just recording a line, one line, for the radio and the circumstances didn't matter, did they?

After the sound file had been sent I sat on, staring at the yellow reams and the violet pens. What would she have made of this moment? Would it have made her squeamish? Probably, I thought; since it had to be done, her position would be, well, what else is there to do but to get on and do it? She could be practical and pitilessly unsentimental when necessary and she had a militant antagonism to habitual practice, to self-enforced behaviour driven by a socially inculcated idea of how one ought to be. One must escape the mesh of the *ought* if possible and be guided by the verbs *need* and *want* and *must*. That had been her lifelong counsel.

I entered her bedroom. Every time I had seen her over the preceding months, she was more etiolated than the time before and this occasion was no exception. This morning she looked particularly dry and fragile, and likely to crumble at the touch. Her breathing, now I was actually in the room, was wavering, pained.

I moved closer. Her mouth was open. Her teeth struck me as huge. I remembered when I looked at my father when he was lying in his bed in the nursing home in Killiney where he had died, thinking the same about his teeth. Of course, neither parent's teeth were different; it was the loss of flesh from their chins and cheeks that was the explanation. The pounds gone, their teeth loomed as never before.

Her eyelids were down but not quite shut. This gave a false impression of consciousness. Her hair, still fine and full, was half white, half auburn. Liver spots on her face and a bruise around the eye and up one side of the forehead. Around the collarbone and lower neck, strange depressions and swellings. Her arms, sticking out of her purple nightdress, were terrifyingly thin. How was it they hadn't snapped? Even the weight of a blanket would break those bones, I thought. Her skin was dry and bumpy, like parchment. She was also cold to the touch (though when I mentioned this and Veronica took her temperature, it was normal). Her posture was ramrod straight – like a figure on a medieval tomb. She was alive – her breathing said that – but her spirit, her Edna-ness, was gone, or at any rate not present.

'Edna, Edna, your son Carlo is here,' Amelia whispered. One eyelid slipped up and a faint smile showed. Her Edna-ness was back. I was sure of it. An extraordinarily small, yet extraordinarily meaningful moment. Then the eyelid dropped, the smile vanished.

Gone again.

Did this actually happen, this moment of presence? We need to be known and seen (and being seen is how we believe we're known). This was so strong a need I'm prepared to believe I made myself believe it happened. The wish was father to the feeling. And yet, and yet. That strange, numinous apprehension that one is in the presence of a living consciousness, it was there for a moment. Could what I was certain I'd felt be something I'd faked? Was my capacity to delude myself so prodigious? Or was it true? I didn't know.

Amelia and Veronica wanted to talk about the bruising on my mother's face, and the shin wound (her leg – was it the left or the right? I can't remember yet I can see the bandages so clearly with my mind's eye now as I write!). As

Amelia and Veronica explained what happened – her homeostatic function got her up in the night and she got entangled with the bars, and all the bars of her bed (they were down now, they were only lifted at night) had bells attached, and as a further precaution there were pressure mats on either side of the bed, which activated an alarm if they were touched – I felt their anxiety. I felt they'd been berated in the past by angry relatives for injuries sustained by old people in their care and they wanted to make sure there was no chance of the pattern (old client, white usually, berating those of colour doing the hard work) repeating. I assured them I didn't doubt them or their competence. The injuries were the consequence of my mother's end-of-life agitation, not their deficiency or negligence.

Because of my current preoccupation with decline, we began to talk about the rise of populism and the growing antagonism shown by people in Britain to people like them. Both began laughing and Amelia said, very carefully, she hoped she was safe to say what she was about to say and she wasn't a hundred per cent sure she was but she was going to say it anyway. And then she said it.

'Mr Farage, Madame Edna doesn't like him. She really doesn't like him. When he comes on the telly she says, "Oh I don't like him. He's a bad man, a very bad man."'

I smiled, I hoped reassuringly.

Emboldened, Amelia continued, 'And there's another man she doesn't like . . .'

'Mr Trump,' I ventured.

'Yes,' she said, 'him. She doesn't like him. But I was thinking of another man . . . Yes . . . Mr Netanyahu. When he's on telly she always says, "Turn it off, I don't want to listen to him. He's a bad man, a horrible man, a wicked man."'

A short pause and then she went on:

'Madame Edna speaks her mind,' said Amelia. 'She speaks her mind. She tells you what she thinks. She doesn't hold back. I went to the Louvre in Paris on my holiday and when I came back and I told her I'd been to the Louvre she said, "What did you go there for? What do you know about paintings? You don't know anything about paintings? There was no point you going to the Louvre, absolutely no point." She was right. I know nothing about paintings and I liked that she said that. I like it when she is forthright, and I like it when she is saying things to me straight. Yes, I like it when she says, "Don't do that, Amelia!" because then I know she's well.'

Veronica asked me to leave. I did. When she had done what she had to do, she called me back. My mother lay in the bed, straight as a poker, unmoving. The soughing of her strained breathing still sounded.

*

The stillness didn't last. She started to kick the bed clothes. She kneaded the air with her hands. She drew her knees up. She pulled at the jersey she wore over her purple nightdress. The agitation was extraordinary, relentless. This was her homeostatic function at work and it had capacity. It sat her up. It swung her legs off the bed. It stood her up. Every time the alarm from the pressure mats went off Amelia or Veronica would rush back, lean in and gently speak.

'Do you want something, Mrs Edna?'

Sometimes they got a whispered word or two and they would know what she wanted but mostly they got nothing. They would lie her back down and she would fall asleep; she would be still for a minute or two and then she would kick off the bed clothes again and she would stand up. This happened many times until eventually she went to sleep.

The hours that followed passed slowly. I sat at the bed by the utterly, abnormally still figure who gave no indication of being alive except by breathing. Sometimes I was alone. I just watched her. To be so estranged from your personhood and so diminished, I thought, was terrible. Sometimes Amelia and Veronica were there and when they were there they talked quietly, stroked her hair and her hands. The hooded eyes stayed down now. There was no recognition of their presence. The carers' lot – massive outflows of attention often for little or nothing in return from the patient – requires unconscionable commitment and fidelity to the caring function, which is one of the best things about human beings, perhaps even the best thing. In the UK, we employ many foreign men and women to do this vital job. They don't get much thanks from us for what they do. Did my mother know she was receiving their kindness? I don't know. I hope she did. What I saw was the best part of the day. I'm sure she would have thanked them if she could. I decided that she would anyway and that made me feel better.

When it was time to go, I stroked her hair and kissed her forehead. An eyelid and another quarter-smile played about her face. Then the eyelid came down and the smile vanished and I left and went out into a tremendous rainstorm.

The next day, back in Fermanagh, I felt bloated with feelings, memories, emotions. I sat mostly and did nothing, I sat waiting and hoping for deflation. It came slowly, like the slowest of slow punctures.

The nights following, I found sleep eluded me. As I lay in bed, I couldn't stop myself listening out for the sound of the phone ringing and then imagining what the voice at the other end would say when I answered. I did fall asleep of course but then I would jerk awake and then again, lying in the dark, ears straining, I'd be listening out for the sound of the phone ringing. I could not shake this pattern.

The Saturday following my return from London, about 5 p.m., the phone rang.

'This is Beatrice,' I heard. 'Will you speak to your mother? She wants to leave here and go home. Perhaps hearing your voice might help her. Don't worry if she gets angry. She's disorientated. She's confused. She says things.'

I agreed.

'Edna,' I heard Beatrice saying, 'it's your son, Carlo.'

'Hello,' I said. (I said this three times.) 'It's me. It's Carlo.'

'Oh . . . Carlo . . .'

'Yes, it's me. How are you?'

'Not good. Terrible.'

'Oh, I'm sorry to hear that.'

'I am in a terrible situation.'

'Oh.'

'I'm being held a prisoner. I'm being held against my will. I want to leave. I want to leave and go home. And if in the next half an hour I'm not released I'm going to call the police. I am. I really am.'

'Can you walk?'

'Yes.'

'Is the sun shining?'

'Yes.'

'Why not ask if you can go out into the garden, so you can sit in the sun?'

'I don't want to go out into the garden. I don't wish to stay here. I want to go home. And I am asking you, Carlo, I am imploring you – please help me. Take me away from here.'

'I can't.'

'Why not?'

'I'm in Ireland, hundreds of miles away.'

'They're holding me prisoner. I will call the police. I mean it.'

Her tone was the adamant tone she adopted in any situation where she wished to suborn. It was the tone that brooked no opposition. It used to make me feel sick, febrile, frightened when I heard it as a child. But under the circumstances under which I was hearing it now, it had a completely different effect. It filled me with pity.

'You know your book, on T. S. Eliot, *The Hermit Thrush*?'

'Yes. I want to finish it.'

'Well, maybe you could work on it today.'

'I don't think so. I must leave. That's what I must do. And you must help me. I need you to help me.'

'I'm in Ireland, another country. I can't just turn up in a taxi and whisk you away. And you can't go home either, you know, to Ovington.'

'Oh yes I can.'

'You can't. You must stay where you are with Beatrice and Amelia and Veronica. You do know that?'

'No. Absolutely not. I won't. I wouldn't. I can't be with them.'

'You can't manage without them.'

'They're holding me prisoner you know.'

Then she listed the names of several other people she might ring.

'Yes, that would be good,' I heard Beatrice saying in the background. 'Why not ring them?'

Beatrice took the phone. 'Thank you, Carlo, thank you.'

A moment later Beatrice sent me a brief WhatsApp. My mother was stronger physically than before but she was disorientated too and she would forget our conversation very soon.

This conversation was the last we had in which *The Hermit Thrush* was mentioned. We never spoke of it again.

Tuesday, 16 July 2024. I woke about a quarter to seven. I let the chickens out and then went back to bed and lay under the hot covers, half-dreaming, half-meditating. I tried to tune in. What exactly was going on within? What came back (this was what I detected) was the usual – anxiety, heaviness, fatigue. I ate breakfast, had a walk. The day began. I finished Henry Green's *Loving*.

This was the junction at which I found myself; it was certain what would happen but when precisely was unknown.

Certainty yoked to uncertainty; uncertainty yoked to certainty. My senses were stretched by this indeterminate way of living. I liked the concrete; I didn't like this. I found myself thinking about the future endlessly. About orphanhood. The idea of my mother as a resource, as a safety net, a last resort, even if never used, had always been there. I had always known I could apply to her for support if something went horribly wrong. After her death the net would be gone, folded up, packed away. What would it mean not to have the fail-safe tucked away at the back of the mind? I couldn't imagine.

Entirely predictably, there was a rise in intrusive thoughts about my own mortality in tandem with these other thoughts. In the past, when I thought about it, death was like something seen through a telescope held to the eye the wrong way. It was there but far away. Now I not only thought about it often but the telescope was the correct way around and I saw my own death, right in front of me. Of course, I didn't like that.

From long exposure to another's long drawn-out expiry, I'd rebounded inwards. Death had returned me to myself, I might say. As a sentient being wasn't that how it always went, or at least should go? Prompted by lived experience, understanding deepens. A parent's approach to death had reminded me of what would happen, in time, to me. This was growth, of a kind.

*

I'd also noticed myself noticing all those little signs which signalled the approach of senescence, the state through which I would pass on the way to extinction. The crick in the small of the back when walking. The effort required rising out of the chair. The difficulty bending down to pick up something that had fallen to the floor. The struggle rising out of bed. The tussle involved in getting feet into socks. All these actions which were once so effortless were no longer so.

The signs and signals of the system's wearing out were many, and suddenly I was noticing just how many there were and how little attention I'd been paying to them. How had I missed these? What have I been doing for the last sixty-nine years? *Drifting about with your head in the clouds rather than facing the facts*, I heard myself saying in my father's peremptory voice.

I popped down to Alison, my next-door neighbour, for a haircut. Her hairdressing salon is attached to the house. A lady with a Polynesian face and the long, bony body of a runner was having her blonde hair straightened, and as this was happening she talked about her children's evening routine.

'Six o'clock it's inside and into the bath,' she said. 'Seven o'clock it's bed. It was the same with me when I was a cub. Six inside and into the bath; seven bed. It was non-negotiable when I was a child and it worked, and I've stuck with it and it's still working with my cubs.'

A lady waiting on the couch with her head in a towel agreed.

'That way you get your evening in,' she said.

'Yes,' said the Polynesian face and then she laughed.

'What are you laughing at?' asked the woman on the couch.

'How I got my evenings in! Oh, I got them in all right.' Her allusion was rich, suggestive. Here was the answer to the question, what is the best way to live? Gorge on pleasure before extinction.

A hairdryer went on. On the floor clumps of hair scurried like mice, moved by the blasts of hot air. The unique hair-and-shampoo smell of the hairdresser's. And the unique female atmosphere too. A memory nibbled. Being taken, as often happened, by my mother when she went to the hairdresser. The wait on a sticky seat (often with a Coca-Cola). The salon's noises and smells; the play of hot water shot from the hand-held hoses, the water gurgling over back-tilted heads, including my mother's, held fast in a porcelain 'U' and then sheeting into the sink below and gurgling away down the plughole while the assistant lathered up the client's hair; women under the humming dryers, which gave them elongated heads like the Mekon, Dan Dare's nemesis, and my mother, as her hair was set, always with a spiral notebook open on her lap, scribbling quickly.

*

As someone is about to die, we involuntarily reach for the life lived. A prophylactic against death. Hello, such memories say to death . . . you have dominion but you can't kill the unbidden memory. It will just come and you cannot stop it.

Two days later, on Thursday 18 July, Amelia wrote to me. 'I just want to update you about Edna,' she began. I knew at once from the tone what would be written below. I read on, of course, and I was right. 'Your mum appears to be deteriorating,' she wrote.

Belfast City Airport. A lot of middle-aged couples (the women in pastel slacks; the men in olive safari jackets). All the couples had excellent glasses and shiny shoes and very good teeth.

At Caffè Nero a man with leather arm patches and the haircut of a Battle of Britain pilot. He couldn't bring himself to touch the keypad when paying. He used the corner of his driving licence to punch in his PIN. A minute later I noticed him fastidiously wiping the table he'd selected with medical wipes.

I sat and tried to prepare. I had been told my mother, who I'd be seeing in a few hours, was sleeping all the time. I had been told she would not recognise me. I found myself wondering if hers was to be the happy death of fable when it finally came. I would have liked it to be and here, self-interest was in play because that's very much what I wanted for myself. We can't think about another human being's suffering without thinking about our own, or at least I can't. I worried hers wouldn't be easy (but didn't know) and so worried mine wouldn't be either.

On the flight I saw what the passengers on either side of the aisle in front of me were watching on their devices. On my right an Indian gentleman was watching footage of the world's most costly wedding (that of Anant Ambani and Radhika Merchant) alternating with TikTok videos of Donald Trump 'dad dancing'. The girl to my left (sundress, brown shoulders, she was straight out of Françoise Sagan's *Bonjour Tristesse)* was watching a live feed of male cyclists streaming across flat plains somewhere in France. She didn't take her eye off the live stream once during the whole flight. Was it her brother or boyfriend who was racing? I wondered.

At Heathrow we had to wait for coaches to take us to the terminal. I reminded myself I must prepare and into my mind barrelled this thought. My actual mother had been taken away and a substitute had been left in her place. The unrecognisable woman I would see in a few hours was a changeling. For an instant this was a serious thought. For an instant I believed it. It was amazing what the mind can do to protect itself.

*

On the train from Heathrow, I sat opposite a man singing bumptiously at the top of his voice. He was belting out Barry Manilow's 'Mandy' (1974), a hit with a supremely banal lyric in which the singer extols Mandy's kissing prowess, berates himself for having sent her packing, and then wishes he could have her back again because nobody can stop him shaking like she can. The words don't cohere yet 'Mandy' has been a standard for decades, I assume with regretful men who favour the song because it allows them to express their sense of having spurned love without having to admit they did.

Whether the singer opposite was part of this cohort I didn't know though I fancied he might be. He was burly. Built like a bouncer. Buzz-cut hair. Hawaiian shirt. His bags were piled on the seats on either side of him. There were people standing and if he'd put the bags on the floor they'd have gladly sat down I imagined but he didn't do that because he didn't want to risk having the wrong kind of person beside him, as I would discover.

At Acton many passengers got off and a Bangladeshi family (eight or nine strong) got on. They sat in the newly vacated seats around me. Hawaiian shirt immediately stopped singing and began flapping his hands in front of his face as if he had just smelt something very unpleasant. There was a stink, rich and rank, his gesture said, and the family who'd just boarded the train were obviously the source. Smelly furriners. No one responded. No one reacted. Everyone just pretended nothing was happening. When he realised he had no supporters, Hawaiian shirt stopped flapping his hands and scowled in all directions. Again, the collective pretended nothing was happening. Hawaiian shirt's scowl gave way to something darker – anger, disgust, contempt. He loudly tut-tutted and shaking his head he stood, grabbed his luggage and moved to the other end of the carriage where he found a seat. Beside me was one of the family who'd got on; female, late teens, early twenties, wearing a long, green, embroidered traditional dress. I had sensed she had watched the scene unfold and that she had sensed my watching it too. We both knew we had seen what we had seen and we had adopted the same strategy; and now Hawaiian shirt was at the other end of the carriage, we turned, as human beings will do, when they have something in common, and I saw she was wearing big Nana Mouskouri glasses which magnified her eyes and I smiled, as if to say, 'I'm very sorry' and she smiled back as if to say, 'Thank you but this is how it goes all the time.'

The last time I visited my mother the tunnels at Hyde Park that took one up to the street were lined with small, stained pillows, which homeless people and buskers had left to bag their spots. There was no sign of these today. I wondered if the council had sent cleaners in who had thrown them away.

The streets above were thronged: tourists, doormen, concierges, chauffeurs. Once I turned off Grosvenor Place, it was quieter; I noticed the flower baskets hanging from the railings, and the lovely pools of floral scent through which I passed as I made my way along the pavement.

Further on, in Belgrave Square, in an act of involuntary prevarication, I stopped to study the memorial to Sir Robert Grosvenor, who built Belgravia. The statue on the pedestal had a rather jaunty-looking Sir Robert with his foot on a milestone reading 'Chester 197 miles'. Sir Robert had been a Member of Parliament, as well as the Lord Lieutenant of the Welsh county of Flint. The statue's pose – informal, nonchalant, Olympian – was meant to communicate a sense of Sir Robert as a restless quasi-buccaneer who had a vision and put it into practice. He created beautiful Belgravia. I didn't find myself being the slightest bit persuaded by this and what's more I resented the attempt to persuade me. Sir Robert, to my mind, was just a lucky man who acquired land through marriage which just happened to be on the outskirts of the capital. Owing to propinquity and good fortune Sir Robert was then able to lay down the lovely stucco houses, which subsequently became the basis for the Grosvenor family's multi-million-pound property portfolio and vast fortune. I used to see London as a place of moods and memories but nowadays I don't. What instead I see is a city which holds in its calcified heart the wealth and values of capital. Once I could tolerate the city's wealth but now I can't as I can only see the damage and hurt the rich of this city have done the poor.

I arrived at my mother's flat. She was in the living room in a chair with a lot of cushions at her back to prop her up. *The Devil Wears Prada* was showing on the television, a film I sensed she'd have hated not that it mattered now. I didn't feel she was following.

The moment at which I arrived coincided with the end of the movie, the part where Anne Hathaway, having declined Meryl Streep's offer to join her world, storms off, throws her phone in a fountain and returns to New York. Here she apologises to her boyfriend and lands the plum job she'd always wanted and becomes a proper journalist. I'd seen the film before and found it mildly amusing but this time round it made me bridle. *How stupid, how trite, how untrue*, I thought. The implication of the film is that by doing the right thing the Hathaway character can secure the future she longs for. It's a ridiculous version of magical thinking. You behave virtuously and the world gives back. In my current state of mind, I had no time or patience for this kind of nonsense. Virtue and good fortune are not connected. Or, to put it differently, the universe was never kind or benign or indulgent. The universe is pitiless. That's the lesson dying teaches.

Amelia turned off the television. I studied my mother. She was even thinner than the last time (just a fortnight ago). As before, the fraught breathing. All the flesh had disappeared from the neck and the larynx and the tendons on either side of the throat stood out like ropes and the voice box above the clavicles looked like a lumpy stone trapped behind her skin.

Amelia fed my mother mango sorbet. Her physical nervous system was still functioning (she would scratch an ear or turn her head, or suck on a straw when it was presented or open her mouth when the spoon with the mango sorbet touched her lips) and, now and again, as the sorbet was fed to her, up would go the eyelids and her two dark eyes would stare out.

On my last visit something had flashed across the face that confirmed, I hoped, that she recognised me. (How strong still the need to be seen, to be recognised.) But this time, nothing like that happened. There was no recognition. Yet I very much felt her eyelids rising were not a purely automatic response. After the eyelids rose up she did see something, but what she saw was not what was around her and in front of her; what she saw was a liminal space between this world and the next. I was sure of this and it gave way (this understanding) to a powerful, uncanny feeling that I was on Earth, beside someone who was also on Earth, but we were in parallel realities, each inaccessible to the other. I couldn't see hers, and she couldn't see mine. I've never had a feeling like it before.

The next day when I arrived at the flat, I found my mother in a white nightdress. She was stretched out on her bed, her stick-like arms lying on the outside of the bedcovers. Veronica had combed her hair and applied lipstick and blackened in her eyebrows. This was in anticipation of our visit. It was not just me but also my cousin Michael who was there.

While she slept, Michael and I talked about the funeral and the arrangements that must be made. Occasionally, my mother scratched herself or tried to kick off the covers and now and again an eyelid or both eyelids went up but again (as yesterday) I felt the eye or eyes that gazed out into the room were not seeing what was in front of her. She was not seeing us. She was seeing wherever she was and that was somewhere else. It was on Earth but far away. The emerald shore? Perhaps, perhaps. Again, the uncanny feeling of two different living realities existing in the same moment in time in the same place, mine and hers. And again, the wanting to know what it was the other saw, and knowing it was impossible to know. That privilege is only for those at their end.

*

When it was nearly time to go, I decided, as this might be the last time I'd see her alive, I'd study her hands and imprint on my memory what I saw. I uncurled the fingers of both and turned them palm up. In childhood I had loved her hands. They were very beautiful, small and smooth, lovely and capable.

She frequently said of herself that she was cack-handed and was no good at doing the sorts of things that one, if one was a female, ought to be good at doing with one's hands. She complained for instance, 'Oh I couldn't sew a button or hem my skirt to save my life.' But there was plenty of evidence to contradict that idea. There was plenty of evidence that she could do terrific things with those hands, which as a child I witnessed. She could write fluently and quickly with them, filling page after page while she muttered under her breath the lines she was writing. (It was as if she was giving herself dictation when she wrote.) With these same hands she could spread tablecloths, set her dining table with plates and cutlery and glasses, arrange flowers, lay and light a fire, plump cushions, straighten rugs, organise shelves, calibrate books, transform rooms. With these hands she could also chop and peel and cook – she was a magnificent cook. There was no end to the brilliant things she could do with her very beautiful and brilliant hands. And looking at them now I saw they were still the small and soft and very shapely hands with the same lines on the palms that I remembered from childhood.

It was then, looking (and trying to imprint their picture in my memory), that I noticed at the wrist, nestled amongst the bones, a small blueish, oyster-shaped bump, though it was smaller than an oyster, pulsing and throbbing. Her pulse. I found it with my fingertips and felt it pushing and fluctuating. It was incredible to feel this organ so forcefully keeping the body alive by circulating the blood even though her spirit, or so I guessed, was gone from this world to some other place.

I did not want to stay in London. Hot, filthy, exhausting. And I had so much to do in Ireland. I was booked to fly home from Heathrow. Departures was rammed. To get into the queue for security, I had to get into a queue. A queue for a queue. Who invented this hell?

Further on, after I'd finally managed to get into security and was waiting in the line for the bag and body search, I noticed a huge red sealing-wax-coloured blob of blood on the grey stone floor. It positively sizzled, this burning red gobbet of blood, and, as the queue in which I waited slowly snaked past it, I couldn't keep my eyes off it.

Later, I came upon a man on the other side of the search area staunching his wrist. I asked him if he was all right. He showed me his wrist. There was a wound. A big, bare gaping wound about the size of a fifty-pence piece. We established that the blood I'd been mesmerised by was his. I asked about his wound. Surely, he needed a doctor. 'It's nothing,' he said repeatedly. 'It's nothing.'

When I arrived home in the late evening and got out of the car at the side of the schoolhouse, something caught my eye. It was an animal outside the door of my study, which is in the old bicycle shed at the top of the playground. It was definitely not a rabbit; I could see that much – but it was about that size. What was it? I crept closer and I saw it was a hedgehog sitting on the mat in front of my study door. I hadn't seen a hedgehog in the garden for twenty years, even twenty-five years. The hedgehogs were all gone. A thought then rose like a bubble from below and popped. *My mother is dead,* I thought, *but she's returned as this beautiful little animal.*

Four days later Beatrice sent a message. My mother was 'a fighter' she said. She was 'in [a] semi-conscious condition but arousable' she said. She had slept all day but when Beatrice had appeared (which was just before writing to me) she had opened her eyes, she said.

This was Thursday. I immediately booked flights to London for the start of the following week.

The next day, Friday, Beatrice wrote again; 'your mum is

now on palliative care'. Her doctor, she added, had been on to the 'Trinity hospice for more end-of-life medication'. Over the preceding months every medical bulletin had been worse than the previous one because that's how it went, and this, I knew, was the last but one.

The literary editor of *The Irish Times*, Martin Doyle, had been in touch by telephone. It was the paper's understanding, he said, that my mother would die very soon (how this knowledge had got to *The Irish Times* and its literary editor I'd no idea and I didn't think to ask; I was also not surprised; everything gets out much more quickly than one imagines) and in anticipation of her death, he said, a supplement was being prepared, which would be published as soon as she died and the paper were anxious that I should contribute. Obviously, the copy was needed immediately.

I am no stranger to compartmentalisation. I have been practising all my life. The conversation with the editor was not conducted by me but by the professional writer called Carlo Gébler and he agreed to the request without demur.

I started to write my piece on the Friday after Beatrice contacted me with the information that end-of-life medication was being sourced by my mother's doctor for her. I made progress. Whatever the circumstances, I have always been able to make progress, I have always been able to write. That is what it is to be a professional writer.

The next day, Saturday, I was interviewed by an Irish journalist about my book, *A Cold Eye*, which was about to be published. As soon as the interview was finished, I went to my study and sat down with the piece I'd written for *The Irish Times*. It was in a rough, first-draft state. I began to comb it through and I was just at the final line when my study door opened and my wife stepped in and said my name. From the way she had materialised and from the tone of her voice as she had said my name and from the way she now stood looking down the room to where I sat at my desk and from the colour of her face I knew immediately. She'd just had a call, my wife explained. From my cousin Michael. He had been with my mother in the flat in London and she had died. I asked about times and worked out by checking her phone it was 4.20 p.m. when she died and I immediately made a note of the time in my diary. It seemed important for some reason to know the exact time, or as exact as it could be got; 4.20 p.m. in the afternoon, that's when she died. Then I went into the house and poured out an Irish whiskey. I drank it in a single gulp. I hadn't had a drink for over a year. I put the bottle away and as I did, on the edge of my mind, the vague thought; she hadn't finished *The Hermit Thrush*. That was a shame but maybe from the pages that remained something might be retrieved.

*

All evening, Act 4, Scene 3 in Shakespeare's *Antony and Cleopatra* was on my mind: soldiers on watch at night hear strange music coming from underground, which they interpret as the god Hercules leaving Antony. Why did this float in? Because it connected me to the question which was moving on the edge of my thoughts? At my mother's end, were there strange noises heard? I wasn't there in the flat in London but I felt sure they might have been.

A day later. Sunday evening. I was unstacking the dishwasher. Thoughts hovering. Into view sidled the question – I wonder if I'll see my mother again? Of course, I would see her; that was what I immediately knew. Absolutely, no doubt about it. But where? Quick as a flash, a composite of all the parties in Numbers 9 and 87 Deodar Road, the two houses my mother owned in Putney and where I lived as an adolescent, appeared before my mind's eye. I saw a coal fire (embers in the grate) and Waterford glasses on a white tablecloth and cutlery and plates and champagne bottles in ice buckets and flickering candles and bowls of French onion soup and guests taking Balkan Sobranie Cocktail cigarettes from glasses and lighting up, and I heard a Richie Havens record playing on the record player, and the hubbub of party chatter. That's how it would be and that's where I would see her, at a party, and this was as certain and true and indisputable as the bowl I held in my hand and was about to stack on top of the other bowls on the top shelf of the Welsh dresser. I've never had a sense that the afterlife and its rewards were true but when I had this vision at this moment there was absolutely no doubt that the future as it would happen was what I had seen.

*

From my journal:

Monday, 29 July 2024
I went to the dentist first thing for a check-up. Oh, I thought, as I climbed the surgery steps to the dentist's front door, last Monday my mother was alive and now exactly a week on, a new Monday, she's not. I imagine my mind will be doing this kind of calculation for quite a while, and I won't be able to stop it.

Tuesday, 30 July 2024
I flew to London.

Wednesday, 31 July 2024
I spent the day clearing the flat where my mother died. I thought of nothing. I felt nothing.

Thursday, 1 August 2024

I got up early to walk to South Kensington Station to catch the Tube to Heathrow. I must have made this journey dozens of times when I came to London to see my mother over the last few years. This morning when I made the journey, I thought, the last time I did this she was alive. Now I make it and she's dead. And for the first time I really felt it, her going. The repeating route brought home her death with a sharpness which until that moment had not hurt me. The knowledge left me anguished.

On the Tube a man sat opposite me eating a stick of celery. The pungent smell of the vegetable (and the snap it made as the man broke it) reminded me of Sunday mornings when my mother made Bloody Marys and served the drinks with long sticks of celery. The Bloody Mary she used to say was 'The best cure going for a hangover.'

When I was in London last week to see her and I was in security at Heathrow I saw a huge gobbet of bright red blood on the grey stone floor. Today, eight days later, I saw a solitary apple, perfect, red, full, juicy – a lovely looking one straight out of *Snow White* – lying on the floor of security. No one picked it up. Everyone stepped around it.

Friday, 2 August 2024
On the first Friday of every month, I am in HMP Hydebank and I was there as usual and the first thing I did was to call up to security to renew my pass. It was a warmish day. There was a smell of stewed tea on the stairs and the special quality of silence that you get in the administration section of every jail I've ever been in. The security office was filled with big men with big belts, heavy handcuffs and retractable batons moving in the stiff manner such men always move in.

I asked politely and I was given my pass and then I left and went down the stairs, retracing my steps in order to go through the turnstiles and on the landings and as I did I thought, Oh I was here on the first Friday in July, and it was warm and there was a smell of tea and that special jail silence and I was making my way down these stairs and my mother was alive, and now a month later she's dead. This was not an anguished or fretful thought but one of those before and after ones I kept having. My mind does love its patterns.

Friday, 9 August 2024 (anniversary of dropping of Atom bomb on Nagasaki)
Vigil in Tuamgraney chapel 5–9 p.m. Drinks and finger food in Nuala's Restaurant afterwards.

Saturday, 10 August 2024
Mass in St Joseph's Church Tuamgraney at 11.00 a.m., followed by the interment on Holy Island.

Throughout my mother's burial on the island, I was filled by the sense that the island, which I knew from childhood, which I had visited in childhood, had been expecting what was underway; I could not shake off the sense that the place had been waiting, holding itself in a state of preparedness, and now the event had finally come to pass, the burial, it was quietly pleased.

When we left the island and were travelling back to the mainland, I was sat in the stern of the boat and sitting there I stared back at the island's shoreline as we moved away and I saw how brilliantly vividly green it was and the thought flashed on me (which hadn't happened on the way to the island when I saw the shoreline was just as brilliantly vividly green): is this the emerald coast?

Sunday, 11 August 2024
Returned home to the schoolhouse with my wife. Bone tired.

Monday, 12 August 2024
The day continues its synchronicity tradition begun years earlier when I read the Laurence Sterne passage in *Tristram*

Shandy that was written on this day, 12 August. Glancing at Richard Fraser's biography of George Barker, *The Chameleon Poet*, I discovered 12 August was the day George Barker wrote in his journal, 'X'd first under the redwoods with the coast of California,' this being the day his relationship with Elizabeth Smart was consummated. The following day he woke to find one of her hairs stuck by his sweat to his shoulder. He took the hair, reverently carried it outside on his palms and laid it down carefully under a tree. Then he returned to his room and typed a letter to Smart telling her he'd found 'the symbol of love' on his shoulder and what he'd done with it.[10] My mother and I often talked about George Barker and Elizabeth Smart (I don't know if she knew either but I know she certainly knew of both of them; and my copy of Smart's account of her relationship with Barker, *By Grand Central Station I Sat Down and Wept*, was my mother's, which had migrated somehow from her shelves to mine, and this is now the copy I use when I teach this text at Trinity). My mother and I never, as far as I remember, talked about George leaving Elizabeth's hair under a tree but it's a detail, I believe, she would have fastened on. I am writing this after her death and I find myself compiling a checklist of other

10 Robert Fraser, *The Chameleon Poet: A Life of George Barker* (London: Jonathan Cape, 2001), p. 157–8.

things that would be of interest to her like George Barker's action; I assume this is a way of keeping a conversation going with the dead.

*

On the first Friday after the funeral, I woke early and asked myself this question: What is it exactly that's going on in my mind? Like Vera Brittain does in *Testament of Youth*, I thought, I must study the mind. I turned my gaze inwards; and this was what I understood:

For years (certainly since her house in Ovington Street caught fire) intrusive thoughts about my mother and her wellbeing had dogged me, making me anxious and fretful. Now the cause of those disabling thoughts was gone but I wasn't feeling lighter. For as one preoccupation had departed, another had replaced it: now, what weighted was the sense of being a solitary. And because it chimed, I found myself returning repeatedly to a passage in John Banville's *The Sea* where Max Morden realises death has marooned him amid an immeasurable sea and, like a latter-day Crusoe, he is utterly alone.

Now the last parent was gone, I, the child, must face the awful truth – I'm next. It's a no-brainer: once the parent dies, the child will be next. Now the bit of cliff that was my mother had gone, I'd been brought up to the edge, or rather the edge had come to me, and from here I looked down on the beating waters surging around the rocks at the bottom of the cliff face onto which I would one day myself plunge.

In the weeks following my mother's death I regularly tried to summon her voice at will and I couldn't; but then while waiting for sleep her voice would just come, clear and bright, lovely and comforting. The memory is such a capacious and magnificent organ, but also such an unbiddable one.

In *Walter Benjamin's Archive: Images, Texts, Signs* I came across a Marivaux quote from *La Vie de Marianne*: why is it we who are limited in so many respects find hardly any limits when it is a question of suffering? This might be glossed: human beings are limited in every way except in their capacity to suffer.

One morning I was in Tesco doing a bit of shopping. I was in the aisle devoted to detergents. Brightly coloured boxes rose on either side and I could smell the special smell of washing powder. I had been up and down this aisle many times over the years I've been visiting Tesco in Enniskillen. On all my hundreds of previous visits I'd felt nothing much except perhaps boredom but this time I was overwhelmed by what I recognised was disgust, pure and unalloyed. I was full of feelings and sorrows, I thought, and yet Tesco was trying to sell me Ariel and Persil! How could Tesco do something as crass as offer the goods (and the goods were identical; only the packaging was different, which added to the insult) it was offering in the hope of getting me to buy them? Had it no conception of what I was feeling? Could it not be understood that a person wrestling with what I was wrestling with should not be harried like this? Did Tesco not know I should not be jostled and preyed upon? That I should be left alone with my feelings?

This sense of a supermarket's indifference to everything I was feeling was followed by the idea that it wasn't just them; no, it was the universe that was indifferent both to her absence and to what I might be feeling and that was what I would have to contend with. And the realisation that this was it forever provoked a never-previously-experienced rage.

Some years ago, my wife sorted out by year all the family photos taken over many decades. And, on the foot of doing that, she has made an album of photographs for each of our children for their thirtieth birthday. In the weeks following the funeral she began making our fourth child's album. In the past I've loved these occasions as they've allowed me to binge on photographs and to revel in the memories they trigger. This year, however, one glance at them and I would turn away. Instead of catalysing memories in which I would lose myself, which was what had always happened before, all the photographs provoked was an exacting but inescapable feeling that I had squandered years, even decades, and I had nothing to show for them. It wasn't true; there were things to show, but the feeling that I'd wasted every opportunity was so strong, it swept everything before it like a flood sweeps everything in front of it and carries all away.

The photographs were also impossible to enjoy because they reminded me of the new anxiety which had arrived since my mother's death – what would my children do when I was gone? I had always been their last resort, I had fondly believed, at least theoretically. Whatever trouble they might find themselves in, I had always been here, and I would never turn them away. But when I was gone, what would they do?

And it didn't stop there. There was more. I had brought them into a world where they were going to die (and they hadn't asked for that, which was a further dereliction on my part) and soon I would absent myself and leave them alone to face the music or the Furies or the worst or whatever. Funnily enough I didn't have the feeling that my mother had abandoned me to this fate. My thinking wasn't nearly so logical. In fact, in general when it comes to her death, my thinking isn't logical. Not at all.

2025

A year or 365 days after my mother died was a Sunday. I had to come to London at short notice and my accommodation – this was unplanned, unintended, completely accidental – was, of all places, in Halkin Street, adjacent to Halkin Place, the site of the block with the basement flat where my mother was at the end and where she died.

I arrived at Heathrow in the afternoon. I took the Tube to Hyde Park Corner; I meandered the familiar tunnels to the street and, as I knew I would, I found myself looking down Halkin Place at the familiar building with the basement flat inside. I looked at my watch: 4.20 p.m. It was exactly a year to the minute since her death. The universe has gone to some trouble to organise this, I thought.

I looked inside myself to see what I was feeling at that moment and, to my surprise, I found that what I was experiencing was the certainty that quietly throbs when one *knows* one is about to see somebody, because you know they are alive and you are alive too. Any moment now I knew, for that was how it went with the eternal, she would emerge through the front door of the block where she had died at 4.20 p.m. on 27 July 2024. And having emerged she would look down the street and she would see me standing where I was, and she would raise a hand in greeting. She too was expecting to see me; indeed, she'd come up from her basement flat and out the door knowing I'd arrived; and a moment after waving, she would begin to totter unsteadily down the street towards me. I knew it. *Amor fati.*